Madrid

320 m / 0.2 miles

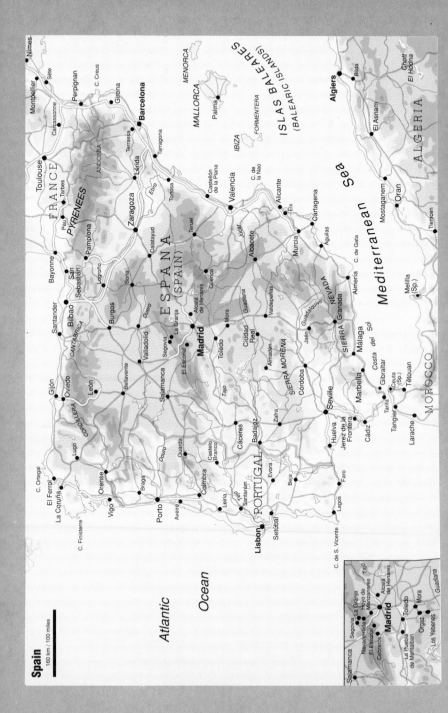

INSIGHT *Pocket* GUIDES

MADRID ←

Written and Presented by **Vicky Hayward**

INSIGHT *Pocket* GUIDES

Insight Pocket Guide:

MADRID

Directed by
Hans Höfer

Managing Editor
Andrew Eames

Photography by
Bill Wassman

Design Concept by
V.Barl

Design by
Carlotta Junger

© 1994 APA Publications (HK) Ltd

All Rights Reserved

Printed in Singapore by
Höfer Press (Pte) Ltd
Fax: 65-8616438

Distributed in the United States by
Houghton Mifflin Company
222 Berkeley Street
Boston, Massachusetts 02116-3764
ISBN: 0-395-68228-2

Distributed in Canada by
Thomas Allen & Son
390 Steelcase Road East
Markham, Ontario L3R 1G2
ISBN: 0-395-68228-2

Distributed in the UK & Ireland by
GeoCenter International UK Ltd
The Viables Center, Harrow Way
Basingstoke, Hampshire RG22 4BJ
ISBN: 9-62421-577-4

Worldwide distribution enquiries:
Höfer Communications Pte Ltd
38 Joo Koon Road
Singapore 2262
ISBN: 9-62421-577-4

BIENVENIDO

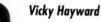

Vicky Hayward

Madrid is a city of extremes: of electrically bright sierra light and deep shadows, freezing winters and sweltering summers, raw dry air and high wide horizons close to the sky. '*Desde Madrid al cielo*', from Madrid to heaven, runs the proverb.

Andalusian poet Antonio Machado described Madrid as 'the breakwater of the 49 Spanish provinces', and indeed the city has remade itself with an astonishing energy since I first came here just over 10 years ago. Now it buzzes with a hard-edged zip to rival Paris or New York and boasts some of the finest art galleries and frenetic nightlife in Europe. But the longer I've lived here, writing about Spain for newspapers and magazines, the more I've become aware of an older city, often just around the corner from slick modern shopfronts, which has kept crumbling plaster, dark bars with hams hanging behind a blaring television, dogs and cologne-soaked children out on the street. When the *Madrileños* look around and say with pride, '*mi pueblo*' — my village — they mean it.

I've tried to capture all sides of Madrid in the itineraries in the book: traditional Madrid, Royal Madrid, Cultural Madrid, Religious Madrid, Bullfighting Madrid — it's all here. Take your pick of what most appeals.

I have got to know this city through my friends, and I am passing on their knowledge to you in this book. I would especially like to thank Juan Datri and Veronica Janssen for their work on the book, and Chitty and Emilio Fernandez, and to Emilio, Marcos and Lola, who first lured me here and have given me more than they will ever know. *Welcome — Bienvenido!*

Contents

Preceding pages:
The Royal Palace

Following pages:
Posters line a café in Toledo

en TOLEDO

TOROS en TOLEDO

Empresa GONZALEZ VERA
Representante FELICISIMO TEJEDOR

FELICISIMO TEJEDOR

● FESTIVIDAD DEL CORPUS CHRISTI

con permiso de la Autoridad y bajo su presidencia, la

ORRIDA DE TOROS

Don Alberto Cunhal Patricio

ESPADAS

ACO   Francisco Rivera

MINO · PAQUIRRI

s cuadrillas de picadores y banderilleros

AS SEIS en punto de la tarde

CAJA DE AHORRO PROVINCIAL DE TOLEDO

60 SUCURSALES EN LA PROVINCIA

su ahorro en "La Caja" beneficia a los toledanos

EL DIA 23 DE MARZO 1975 ● Domingo de Ramos

se verificará, si el tiempo no lo impide, con permiso de la Autoridad y bajo su presidencia, la

¡TRADICIONAL CORRIDA DE TOROS!

6 Soberbios Toros de Don JOSE y Don FRANCISCO ORTEGA SANCHEZ, para

CURRO ROMERO
RAFAEL de PAULA
PACO ALCALDE

Acompañados de sus correspondientes cuadrillas de picadores y banderilleros

La corrida empezará a las CINCO en punto de la tarde

DESPACHO DE LOCALIDADES, a partir del Jueves día 20 en TOLEDO, en las ofici-
nas y en MADRID, en el BAR LAS PANDERETAS, Jardines
ABUNDANTE SERVICIO DE AUTOCARES CON BILLETES DE IDA Y VUELTA   ESPECTACULO NUMERO 17

FUTBOL - Campo Municipal - Toledo
EL DOMINGO, 23 DE MARZO - A las DOCE de la mañana REAL MADRID - C. D. TOLEDO

HISTORY &

Madrid is one of Europe's youngest capitals. 'If you wish to conserve your dominions,' Charles V advised his son Philip II, 'leave the court in Toledo; if you wish to increase them, move it to Lisbon; if you do not mind losing them, take it to Madrid.' Philip ignored his father's advice and in 1561 moved the cumbersome court from the great city of Toledo to the dusty crossroads town of Madrid.

At the time, Madrid was an agricultural hill-town of some 20,000 people – a third the size of Segovia and a quarter of Toledo – with a reputation for quality wheat, wine and cheese. Its history

Philip II moved the court to Madrid

reached back only to the 9th century, when a fortress was built here to guard the mountain passes to Toledo. The Muslims gave Madrid its name – 'Mayrít', or 'running waters', referring to its abundant springs and streams – and a maze-like urban layout.

For several centuries after Alfonso VI's conquest of Mayrít in 1083, the city remained a hybrid Christian-Muslim satellite to Toledo. It kept its Arab name as well as 'Magerit', the Castilian version, but now the large and wealthy Muslim and Jewish communities lived and exercised their trades outside the walls.

As the fortress town grew into a thriving agricultural and trading community, *arrabales* – new

Culture

quarters outside the wall — mushroomed. Madrid's rise was marked by the granting of its *fuero*, a town charter laying down citizens' rights and duties (beard-pulling, swearing, and knife-carrying were punishable offences); and by new walls in the 12th and 15th centuries. It was Charles V, cured of a long illness here, who gave Madrid its title *Villa Imperial y Coronada* (imperial and crowned town), and who chose Madrid's Alcázar or fortress as a residence for his son, the crown prince Philip.

Madrid of the Austrias

But the town was pitifully ill-equipped to cope with the arrival of the Habsburg court, which brought in its wake the paraphernalia of state and empire, plus courtiers, diplomats, bankers, artists, monks and thieves. Within 40 years the population multiplied five times to reach 100,000. This first deluge shaped much of Madrid's character. Even today most *Madrileños* were born elsewhere, making their city a mirror of Spanish regionalism.

Sixteenth-century Madrid mapped out

The Plaza Mayor around 1700

The sudden nature of Madrid's birth also made it a capital of extremes. 'Of Madrid, heaven and earth,' as Cervantes put it. The court's ostentation set a taste for grandeur and conspicuous consumption still evident today. Mule and horse trains loaded down with wine and food for the court rolled in daily, as do today's lorries, from all points around the country. Masquerades, bullfights – then on horseback – royal welcomes, and a string of other fiestas were held in the purpose-built Plaza Mayor. Ever anxious to keep their influence at court, the Church had its own spectacles, such as canonisations (the first was of San Isidro, Madrid's patron saint) and *autos-da-fe* (sacramental plays).

At the same time, handicapped by the lack of a navigable river and by the monarchy's lack of encouragement, Madrid produced almost nothing economically. Chronic unemployment made roguery a way of life and, away from the court and the nobles' houses, convents and monasteries, the majority lived in endemic poverty, lacking the most basic foodstuffs. Despite a new wall built in 1625, overcrowding was so bad that many lived in basements described by an Italian traveller as 'the architecture of moles'. What most called visitors' attention was the sewage chucked out of the windows after 10 o'clock at night, with a cry of *'¡agua va!'* to give passers-by time to get out of the way. There was no street lighting except on the occasional religious shrine, and no rubbish collection.

The noble Madrid of the Austrias also remained a makeshift city. It had no cathedral or university, and few medieval monuments, except for two bridges against the river's flash-floods. Philip II's energies and vision were expended on the austere palace-mausoleum of El Escorial, outside Madrid. Even in the next century, after the court was a permanent fixture, the style remained plain, mixing cheap brick with expensive stone from the sierra to frame doors and windows fronted by iron railings. Today these classically proportioned buildings have a rigorous beauty. Only in the mid-17th century did the city have an ornamental outburst, *madrileño* baroque, in which rich decoration was set against schematically plain backgrounds under slate roofs.

The tensions between society's grandiose facade and the crumbling decadence behind it were caught by the writers of Spain's Golden Age: Calderón de la Barca, Lope de Vega, Tirso de Molina, and Quevedo, all educated at the Imperial Jesuits' School but who wrote for a theatre tradition as popular as today's cinema. Royal patronage also made the city a magnet for outsiders: among them, Miguel de Cervantes, whose masterpiece *Don Quixote* satirised the old courtly values, and Diego de Velázquez, whose portraits at court capture the dying imperial age of Spain more powerfully than any words.

Age of Enlightenment

The change of dynasties in 1701, after Charles II died without an heir, ushered in many changes. The Bourbons, still on the throne today (although toppled and restored three times in the intervening centuries) brought with them a centralised reforming monarchy and French 18th-century magnificence to oust Habsburg spiritual austerity. Among the early Bourbons, Charles III, affectionately nicknamed the 'king-mayor', left a particularly strong mark on Madrid. Streets were paved, cleaned and lit. Begging and gambling were controlled and the famous *serenos*, or night-watchmen, of Madrid were introduced.

Charles III and his successors were also responsible for giving Madrid its heavily classicist monumentalism: the old post office in the Puerta de Sol, the Astronomic Observatory, Puerta de Alcalá, Hospital de Carlos III (now housing the Reina Sofia art centre), Hospicio de San Fernando (now the Municipal Museum), the Conde Duque military barracks and the tobacco factory all date from this time, their original functions reflecting the state's new role in the Age of Enlightenment. The single greatest architectural bequest was the layout of the Paseo del Prado as a social cat-walk and centre of learning, a street which steadily accumulated artistic riches that have made it Madrid's greatest show-place.

Whilst Madrid was thus becoming a European capital, it was also developing its own *castizo* culture (*see p. 25*), observed by the painter Goya. Anti-Europeanism showed itself in the 1766 revolt against a ban on the cape and sombrero – in reality a move against crime – and came to a head more

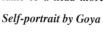

Self-portrait by Goya

seriously after the French Revolution, when Ferdinand VII opened the door to Napoleon and ordered the royal family into exile in 1808. This triggered the spontaneous 2nd of May uprising, bloodily put down but fervently adopted since as a symbol of the *Madrileños'* spirit of unbowed popular heroism. During the rest of the French occupation Napoleon's brother, nicknamed Pepe Botella – literally Pete the Bottle – tried in vain to woo support by laying on fiestas and bullfights and removing taxes on alcohol (hence his nickname), but in vain.

The restoration of the Bourbon monarchy did not bring the hoped-for calm after the storm. Ferdinand VII's court sent many, including Goya, into exile, and Spain swung between absolutism and constitutionalism – a lasting legacy from the ideas of the French Revolution – throughout the 19th century. It was only the signing of the Constitution in 1876, during Alfonso XII's reign, which marked peace for Madrid.

During that time Madrid remained a largely medieval city to outsiders' eyes, closing its gates at 11pm in summer and even keeping part of its walls until 1871. The ever cynical writer Richard Ford commented: 'The walls ... are of mud, and might be jumped over by a tolerably active Remus; but they were never intended for defence against any invaders, except smuggled cigars.' Washington Irving's impression was also of a capital remote from the rest of Europe. Like other Romantic travellers, he saw local habits, such as the siesta – often taken in the street – food-vendors and farmyard animals, the evening *paseo*, women's *mantillas* and fan-language as the exotica of a southern city.

Seeds of Modernity

In fact the seeds of modernity were sown in this period. Migration from country areas hit by chronic unemployment and periodic famine took the population from 170,000 in 1800 to 500,000 by

Goya's 'Execution of the Rioters' commemorates the 1808 uprising

the end of the century, and it doubled again by 1930. Alongside this came the first timid signs of late industrialisation – shoe, textile and tobacco factories – and the arrival of the railway, gas street-lighting and running water. To the east of the extending Paseo de Castellana, the Marquis of Salamanca developed the quarter of the same name while liberal reformers created the garden suburb of Ciudad Jardín to the north of that.

The speed of change quickened in the 20th century. In 1910 Gran Vía, the city's first high-sided commercial avenue, cut a swathe through the old town, and in the following 30 years, the Metro and radio arrived and Barajas airport was built. Nevertheless, Madrid remained a relaxed capital, drawing outsiders into its nightly café *tertulias*, open literary and artistic conversations, in which Buñuel, Dalí and Lorca loomed large in the 1930s.

The *Madrileños* also witnessed the century's most important national political events: the loss of the overseas colonies in 1898, the proclamation of the republic and the royal family's exile in 1931, the revolution and general strike of 1934, and the beginning of the civil war in July 1936. For three years, Madrid suffered hunger, Nationalist bombardments and alarms, and families were divided by their ideology: the raised arm on the statue of Don Quixote in the Plaza de España was said by nationalists to be giving the salute and by communists to be ordering them to storm the prison. These divisions were to leave deep and long-lasting scars.

During the years of hunger, or *años de hambre*, after the war recovery was slow. At that time, Franco's Madrid embodied the most conservative aspects of his centralist dictatorship. The city became closed to European ideas, and many who were against the regime went into exile. Camilo José Cela wrote of 'whole streets of a sinister gaze, with the appearance of lodging men without conscience'.

But from the early 1950s, society was changing radically under the surface. Franco began building up Madrid's industry into what is now the biggest concentration in Spain, and at the same time the increasing importance of transport networks began to show the benefits of Philip II's decision to have a dead-central capital. The city grew again, but with visually archaic taste: first, neo-Habsburg brick buildings around the bombed western fringes of town; then high-rise concrete and glass blocks in place of old palaces on the Paseo de Castellana; and, on the edges of the city, shanty-towns without running water or plumbing. Towards the end of the dictatorship Madrid also became a major centre of political opposition, focused on the universities and the unions.

Movida and Money

When Spain finally emerged from dictatorship after Franco's lingering death in 1975, the pent-up desire for change spun Madrid into two decades of dizzying transformation. Proof that the young democracy was rooted – and that the constitutional monarch, Juan Carlos I, had a crucial role to play – came in 1981, after the failure of an attempted military coup.

Madrid's remaking of itself as a democratic capital rather than a court city owed much to one man: Enrique Tierno Galván, the first socialist mayor, whose 25-year plan encouraged both the recuperation of popular traditions and youth culture, which exploded in the iconoclastic *Movida*. Out of *Movida* came fashion and art magazines, rock groups and urban tribes, a frenetic migratory nightlife, much fake liberalism and sexual hedonism, plus the odd genuine vein of creativity, most notably the films of Pedro Almodovar.

Underpinning all this, especially from 1984, was rapid economic growth, which in the late 1980s became the fastest in Europe. Accompanied by an influx of foreign investment, it gave Madrid a hard-edged money culture, wealthy new suburbs, its own jet-set and one of the highest costs of living in the world. One side-effect of growth outrunning the infrastructure has been chronic traffic congestion, now the city's main problem.

A frenetic nightlife

More positively, the boom released large sums for a major urban face-lift, interesting new architecture and investment in cultural assets. Outsiders also notice the parallel blossoming of local pride. As a car sticker puts it: *Ser español un orgullo, ser Madrileño un titulo.* 'To be Spanish a pride, to be *Madrileño* a title.'

But for all the brassy gloss, Madrid remains an insecure capital. The urge to make up for lost time is almost tangible. The city strives to be dynamic; *Madrileños* are as keen to score points on the political, business and cultural circuits as in football leagues.

It is ironic, then, that Madrid's appeal to outsiders is not its slick new face, but the traces of an older way of life. The importance of local drama and gossip; the energy of life within the *barrios*; the formal details of dress and *politesse*; the *Madrileños'* references to *mi pueblo*, my village – all these come naturally here. It is the cheek-by-jowl coexistence of the traditions of the old and the dynamism of the new which makes Madrid what it is: restless and tireless, visually kinetic, maddening one moment and magical the next. And always a case apart.

Historical Highlights

854 Foundation of 'Mayrít' (Madrid) by Mohammed I near previous prehistoric, Iberian and Roman and Visigothic settlements.

1083–86 Alfonso VI captures Mayrít from the Arabs.

1085 Alfonso VI conquers Toledo.

1109 Alif Ben Yusuf sacks, but does not take, Madrid.

1202 Alfonso VIII sanctions *Fuero de Madrid*, formalising town laws and rights.

1309 Ferdinand IV holds first Cortes in Madrid.

1369 Trastamara dynasty begins; Henry II enlarges the Alcázar.

1465 Henry IV gives Madrid the title 'very noble and very loyal'.

1474 Isabella I of Castile León and her husband Ferdinand of Aragón (the Catholic Kings) take Madrid and move Crown Treasury there.

1480 Inquisition established in Castile.

1492 Expulsion of Jews.

1516–55 Charles I of Spain, Holy Roman Emperor, rules Spain from itinerant court, opening Habsburg dynasty.

1520 Revolt of Commons.

1561 Philip II moves court from Toledo to Madrid.

1563–84 Building of El Escorial.

1547 Birth of writer Miguel de Cervantes.

1601–6 Court moves to Valladolid, but returns permanently to Madrid.

1609 Expulsion of *moriscos* (converted Muslims).

1619 Completion of Plaza Mayor.

1621–65 Reign of Philip IV.

1625 Work begins on building Madrid's fourth city wall (it lasts till 1860).

1632 The Palace of Buen Retiro is built.

1599–1660 Diego de Velázquez, painter.

1700–13 Victory of Philip, Duke of Anjou, in War of Spanish Succession opens the Bourbon dynasty.

1737–1764 Building of new royal palace on the site of the Alcázar, after it was burned down.

1746–1828 Francisco Goya, painter.

1759–83 Charles III, the 'mayor-king'; extensive building in Madrid.

1800–1900 Madrid's population grows: 170,000 to 500,000.

1808 Charles IV abdicates and French army enters Madrid; on May 2 Madrid rises against the French but is brutally quashed.

1808–14 War of Independence (Peninsula War), during which Napoleon's brother, Joseph Bonaparte, rules. The French are defeated.

1814–33 Ferdinand VII; restoration of Bourbon dynasty.

1836 and **1855** Disentailment of religious property.

1851 First train service from Madrid to Aranjuez.

1910 Building work begins on the Gran Vía.

1919 Metropolitano, the underground system, opens.

1931–36 Second Republic declared, following abdication of Alfonso XIII.

1936–39 Spanish Civil War.

1939–75 General Francisco Franco rules; city population grows from 1 to 3 million.

1975 Juan Carlos I succeeds Franco; restoration of Bourbon monarchy.

1978 Crown guarantees constitution granting autonomy to regions.

1979 First democratic municipal elections: Enrique Tierno Galván is elected mayor of Madrid.

1981 Attempted military coup fails after congress held at gunpoint.

1986 Spain joins the European Community.

Day itiner

Sign language

Madrid is a compact capital, but its small, adjacent *barrios*, or neighbourhoods, have very distinct personalities. The itineraries I have assembled in the following pages are designed with this in mind, since it is easy to hop from one *barrio* to another and the contrasts between them – old and new, popular and elegant – are the key to the city's character. The itineraries are also designed to highlight what the city offers best. Two things should not be missed: the visual arts and the nightlife.

The itineraries fit around the Spanish day: that is, a long morning until lunch around 2–3pm, after which many – although not all – museums, monuments and workplaces are shut. Eating earlier than 2 or 3pm blocks out several of the few available hours for sightseeing or shopping. For the same reason, the itineraries tend to be busier in the mornings than the afternoons. If you get into Spanish habits – that is lunch as the main meal of the day and long, late nights – you may want the afternoons for siestas.

Moving about in Madrid can be difficult. A car is a positive liability since the city is traffic-choked, and also unnecessary because it is so compact. Walking is often quicker – and more pleasant – than taking buses or taxis. It helps to remember that all street numbering is from the Puerta del Sol outwards. Abbreviations commonly used on maps are **C** (*Calle*), **Av** (*Avenida*), **Trv** (*Travesia*), **P** (*Puerta*), **Pl** (*Plaza*) and **Ctra** (*Carretera*).

Madrid is a good springboard for visiting the old cities of Castile. I have limited myself to places that can be seen within a day, with suggestions of how you might like to extend trips if you have time.

Castizo Madrid

The old town's three main squares – Puerta del Sol, Plaza Mayor and Plaza de la Villa – and the Convento de las Descalzas; in the afternoon, a tour of late 19th-century Madrid; and in the evening 'tapas' in theatreland.

– Starting point: Metro Sol –

The **Puerta del Sol** is not Madrid's most beautiful square, but it is the city's heart, both literally – all distances in Spain are measured from *Kilómetro 0*, marked by a pavement plaque in front of the clock-tower – and as the best place to measure the city's pulse. The bullfighting touts, shoppers, buskers and lottery-ticket sellers make a kinetic tableau of Madrid's street life. As Pérez Galdós wrote in the 19th century, here '*se cruzan las ansiedades; la sangre social entra y sale, llevando las sensaciones o sacando el impulso*' ('anxieties/beliefs meet; society's blood comes and goes, heightening your sensations or draining your strength').

The square was rebuilt in the mid-19th century around the red-brick post office (1756) – now police station – and its name is the only reminder of the city gate decorated with a carved sun (*sol*), which stood here till the 16th century. But the square has many other associations. One is the 2 May 1808 uprising, when *Madrileños*, poorly armed with guns, knives, and bricks and furniture to throw out of windows,

In the Puerta del Sol

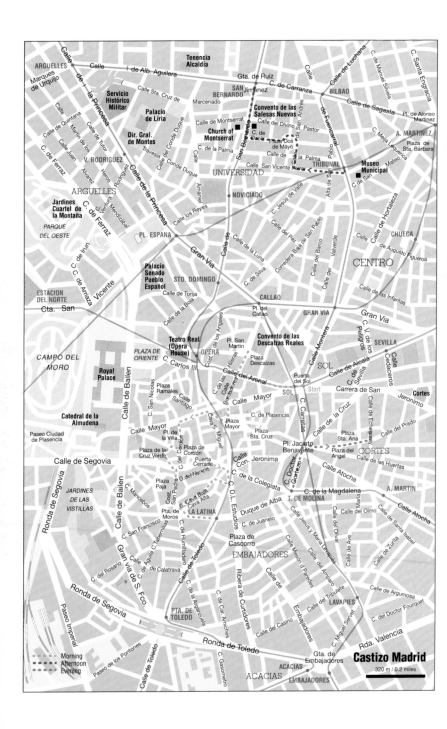

Castizo Madrid

320 m / 0.2 miles

Morning
Afternoon
Evening

fought on the streets against the occupying French; the following day, hundreds of Spaniards were shot here in cold blood, a horrific scene immortalised by Goya.

Closer memories are of the Franco years, when many people spent at least a night in the police station. Today, though, the main association is happier. On New Year's Eve thousands gather here to gobble down a dozen grapes – one for each month – as the ball in the clock-tower drops and midnight chimes.

Taking Calle del Arenal out of the *plaza* (Pastelería Mallorca, on the corner, makes a good stop-off for coffee and cake), it's a 5-minute walk, via Calle San Martín, second on the right, to the **Convento de las Descalzas Reales**, literally Convent of the Barefooted Royals (Tuesday to Thursday 10.30am–12.30pm and 4–5.30pm; Friday 10.30am–12.30pm; Sunday and holidays 11am–1.30pm; fee; 50-minute guided tour).

A small corner of the past preserved within high walls, and many *Madrileños'* favourite monument, the convent was founded in 1564 by Charles V's daughter, Joanna of Austria, in the palace where she was born. The painted staircase, frescoes, shrines and works of art given in lieu of the blue-blooded nuns' dowries condense the richness of Spain's Golden Age. It is still a working convent, and the kitchen garden is said to produce the most expensive vegetables in Spain, such is the value of the land. Unfortunately, the rest of the square is a mess; the splendid Renaissance doorway on the savings bank was moved here from elsewhere.

Inside the Convento de las Descalzas

Going back down Calle San Martín, then straight over Calle Arenal, down Calle Bordadores, crossing over Calle Mayor and up Triunfo, you emerge in the **Plaza Mayor**, the centre of Habsburg Madrid and a mirror of its social life. The café terraces make good pews, but you pay in the price of your drink; sitting on the benches and leaning against the lampposts is free.

The current *plaza* dates from the end of the 18th century after a fire swept through the earlier wooden buildings in 1790, but its roots go back much further, to the Arab *zoco*, or souk, which grew up on the site of a dried-up lake. The first building was the **Casa de Panadería** (1590, now rebuilt), from which the guild of bakers

Casa de Panadería

controlled the prices and consumption of cereals; then, in 1619, Philip III – whose statue stands in the centre of the square – ordered the *plaza* to be built, for markets and fiestas. It could accommodate up to 100,000 people. The height – six storeys – was revolutionary at the time, inspiring a wave of jokes about people living on top of each other.

For all the transformations it has undergone, the Plaza Mayor has kept its popular character. Today, the most striking new features are the Panadería frescoes, finished in 1992, which show Cibeles, goddess of Madrid, looking for her daughter Proserpine in the underworld. Brilliantly coloured, the semi-erotic images are more 1980s than baroque and full of allegorical detail: white cats on the towers represent the *Madrileños* who, according to legend, shinned up walls and over roofs to conquer Muslim Madrid.

Strolling out of the arches around the square, you get intriguing glimpses of old Madrid. Off the southeastern corner stands the **Carcel del Corte** (1629), today the Ministry of Foreign Affairs, one of the key examples of Habsburg court architecture. Off the other eastern corner, shops in Calles Sal and de las Postas have wonderful arrays of underwear, flamenco costume, cloth for religious brotherhoods, and fluorescent cribs. Finally, the western corner adjacent to Calle Mayor brings you out by the Mercado San Miguel, a wonderful 19th-century iron and glass market with everything from fruit to ironmongery, and a local coffee bar.

Heading on from here down the Calle Mayor, you come to the **Plaza de la Villa** (laid out in 1463), the medieval centre of government. Originally called the Plaza de San Salvador, after a long-gone church where the medieval council met, the square's eastern side (on the left as you face it) keeps Madrid's two

Doors of the Torre de los Lujanes

oldest buildings: the **Torre de los Lujanes**, a 15th-century brick *mudéjar* tower with bands of masonry, big wooden beams (heavily restored at the beginning of the century), horseshoe arches and a splendid Gothic door. Inside the corner door beyond are the splendid tombs of Beatriz 'La Latina' Galdona, Isabel of Castile's brilliant Latin tutor, and her husband; further in is a carved stone staircase built by Moslem artisans for the hospital founded by La Latina, which gave its name to one of the city's quarters.

The other buildings in the square were rebuilt in the 16th and 17th centuries with what was seen as more appropriate grandeur: on the south side, the **Casa de Cisneros**, with a magnolia in the courtyard, which replaced the old butchers' guild; on the west side, the **Casa de la Villa** (1640–92) replacing the granary-turned-prison. Today these are occupied by departments of the town hall, but uniformed porters give them an old-world feel.

From here, a 20-minute walk down through old Madrid takes you to lunch in one of its taverns. Leaving from the back of the square through the narrow Calle del Cordón – filled by the smell of baking from the kitchen of the nearby convent – jink right at the end, go past the splendid Renaissance facade at the back of the Palacio de Cisneros to a post-modern *plaza*, then take the first left down Calle del Rollo, a former parish boundary, to Plaza de la Cruz Verde, where the last Inquisition burning took place. These quiet streets give a glimpse of Madrid's humble, 17th-century, plaster-and-beam architecture – such as the Casa de Juan Vargas (San Isidro's employer), on the left as you enter the Plaza de Cordón and the *casa de la malicia* at the bottom of Calle del Rollo. Alongside this are the grander brick and stone buildings of the nobility, and the more ornate 18th- and 19th-century palaces.

From the Plaza de Cruz Verde, turn left briefly up fume-filled Calle Segovia and then right up Calle San Pedro, and immediately turn left again down Calle del Nuncio, with its old palaces and

> ### Castizo
>
> *Castizo*, meaning pure-blooded or authentic, is used to describe anything which captures the *madrileño* character. Its use dates back to the 18th century, when, despite enormous poverty, *Madrileños* developed a cheeky swaggering style, dressing more elegantly than they could afford and using exaggerated slang incomprehensible to the outsider. The spirit of this historic *castizo* is well caught in the 19th-century *zarzuelas*, or operettas, and the spring and summer *verbenas* – street-fiestas – for which older people don the traditional costume – checked caps and waistcoats for men, and headscarves plus shawls over long spotty dresses for women – to dance the *chotis*.
>
> More fundamentally, the *castizo* character, which has risen above hardship and even tragedy with humour and bravura, gives Madrid's street-life its wit and cut-and-thrust drama. Quick to take offence, *Madrileños* are rarely short of a sharp-tongued ironic retort or roguish facial expression. This street-cockiness is popularly known as *chulería*, which film director Luis Buñuel defined as 'typically Spanish, made up of aggression, virile insolence and self-sufficiency'.

Tiled facade of Laboratorios Juanse in Malasaña

seigneurial houses. You come out at **Puerta Cerrada**, so called because the city gate there was kept closed against bandits and smugglers of wine from Valdepeñas. No surprise, then, that it's a traditional centre of bars and restaurants. The most traditional for an *aperitivo* and *tapa* of *jamón* or cheese (though not cheap) is **Casa Paco**, Pta Cerrada 11.

From here, you can smell the woodsmoke puffing out of Cava Baja, once a defensive ditch outside the city wall. The old coaching inns specialising in wood-oven roasts, which grew up here on the edge of town, have recently made a big comeback. **Posada de la Villa** is one of the best; or, if you don't feel like a big meal, **Maxi**, Cava Alta 4, is an excellent traditional tavern where you can have a single dish.

After lunch, you may well want to succumb to a siesta. Alternatively, revived by a coffee, look at a younger, but equally characterful, part of town. A short ride on the Metro (Latina to Tribunal) will bring you out opposite the **Museo Municipal**, Calle Fuencarral 98 (10am–2pm and 5–9pm; free admission), once the city's orphanage. Its wildly ornate baroque doorway depicts San Fernando, patron of orphans. Behind it the museum displays take a light look at Madrid's history, from mammal's bones found en route by the river to the 20th century city, passing

---

A Short Castizo Dictionary

Chotis: Slow mazurka danced to the barrel-organ in a straight-backed, sedate style, in which the couple's feet should apparently effortlessly remain within the space of a brick.

Chulo: Flashy, slick; also a pimp or gigolo. A *chulapona* is the female equivalent.

Chulear: To tease or insult jokingly.

Chulería: Typically *madrileño* all-knowing attitude towards life.

Finolis: Someone trying to be elegant and 'señorito'.

Lechugino: A lightweight fake, a bluff or dandy (literally a lettuce character).

Piropo: or *requiebro*, flirtatiously flattering comment.

San Isidro: Madrid's patron saint, a farm labourer canonised along with his wife, whose feast-day is celebrated in May.

Verbena: Popular street-fiestas usually on saints' days, with games, food, and plenty of drink.

a great model of the 17th-century city, maps and paintings.

From here, **Calle San Vicente Ferrer**, almost opposite, takes you into Malasaña – previously Maravillas – a 19th- and early 20th-century *barrio* with flower-filled balconies, small shops and a lot of bars. It has kept some of its hand-tiled facades: the most amusing are Laboratorios ' Juanse' and the Antigua Huevería, at No 28, both on the corner with Calle San Andrés. Also well preserved is the **Casa do Campaneiro**, a Galician bar at No 44 opposite a tattoo shop, where you can have coffee or wines by the glass.

Taking Calle San Andrés, you pass the facade of La Industrial, an old *neo-mudéjar* ice factory, as you slope down to the **Plaza Dos de Mayo**, once the gardens of a palace and another flashpoint of the 1808 uprising against the French. It was here, in the artillery barracks, that Manolita Malasaña, aged 17, after whom the *barrio* was named, helped her father and the other troops load guns for the defence of the barracks, until she was shot down by French bullets.

From here, it's a five-minute walk up Calle Daoiz to San Bernardo, once a university area and the home of noble families, though their palaces are now occupied by institutions. Opposite is the church of Montserrat (1640), with its famous tower by Pedro Ribera, baroque architect. On the same side of the street, at No 35, you can buy delicious cakes made by the nuns at **Las Salesas Nuevas** convent (9am–1.30pm and 4.30–9pm). And now return to your hotel for a rest.

In the evening, head for the **Plaza Santa Ana** (Metro Tirso de Molina), the centre of theatreland. Redolent with bullfighting associations – Hemingway used to hang out in the **Cervecería Alemana** (No 6) – this is one of the classic quarters to go out for *tapas*. The most picturesquely tiled bar in the city, **Los Gabrieles** (Echegaray 7), is good place with a *fino* or dry sherry. A route around half a dozen bars with different specialities is given on page 70, or do it the Spanish way and try places that catch your eye in any of the side streets. If you would prefer a meal instead – or as well – there is a great spread of regional restaurants around Calle Echegaray.

The Plaza Dos de Mayo

After that, if you have the energy, there are plenty of nightlife options within a stone's throw: jazz at the **Café Central**, classical music at **La Fídula**, or, from around 1–2am, the **Villa Rosa** discotheque (*see pp. 75–6 for addresses*).

Royal Madrid

In the morning, allow 3 to 4 hours to visit the Royal Palace, or its quarter; after lunch, 2 hours to walk with 'Madrileños' in the Retiro Park and, if you have the energy, another 2 hours in the stunning Thyssen Museum before cocktails and dinner.

Philip IV in bronze

– Starting point: Metro Opera –

By the 17th century, Madrid had two splendid royal residences: to the east, the Retiro Palace, of which only the gardens remain; to the west the Alcázar, today's Royal Palace, which was rebuilt with Bourbon magnificence in the 18th century. Both enjoy wide horizons where you can appreciate Madrid's dramatically lit skies.

You reach the **Royal Palace** from Plaza Isabel II, dominated by the vast **Teatro Real** (Opera House), built in 1808. It is finally due to open in 1995 after long years of closure under Franco, and more of building work (the stage-tower is taller than the Eiffel tower). If you need breakfast, take the Calle de Arrieta to the **Taberna del Alarbadero**

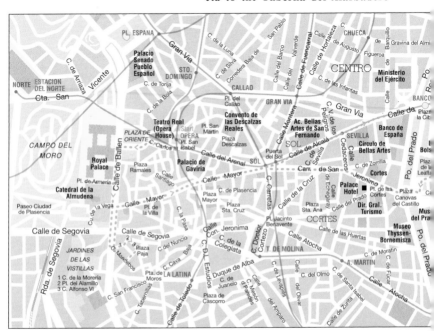

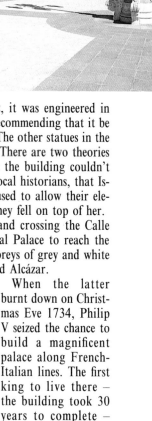

(Calle Felipe V 6), owned by a priest. Otherwise, take the Calle Carlos III to pop out into the **Plaza de Oriente** facing the palace's huge grey facade.

For two centuries after the current palace was built, the main feature of the half-moon *plaza* was the Caños del Peral, a fountain fed by underground waters. Before that, though, it was one of the main focuses of the city: excavations have so far turned up the royal treasury, library, other government departments, parts of the Arab Alcázar and even a Visigothic settlement.

In the centre of the *plaza* stands the 8,150-kg (18,000-lb) equestrian bronze of **Philip IV**, the first statue to solve the difficulties presented by a horse rearing up on its back legs. Designed by Velázquez, it was engineered in Italy, where Galileo solved the problem by recommending that it be made hollow in front and solid at the back. The other statues in the square were made for the top of the palace. There are two theories why they never made it up there: one, that the building couldn't support their weight; the other, backed by local historians, that Isabel de Farnese, Philip V's second wife, refused to allow their elevation after she had a nightmare in which they fell on top of her.

Walking down the centre of the square and crossing the Calle Bailén, you pass the east facade of the Royal Palace to reach the Plaza de Armería. The present palace, six storeys of grey and white stone, was built from 1735 to replace the old Alcázar.

When the latter burnt down on Christmas Eve 1734, Philip V seized the chance to build a magnificent palace along French-Italian lines. The first king to live there – the building took 30 years to complete – was Charles III and the last was Alfonso XIII, who moved out when he abdicated the throne in 1931. In the interim, the *plaza* was where the monarchy and entourage showed themselves to their

Royal Madrid

320 m / 0.2 miles

people. Here the Italian princess María Antonia de Borbón had her first meeting with her husband Ferdinand VII, about whom she wrote home: 'I thought I would faint. In the portrait he looked rather ugly. Well, compared to the original, the portrait was of an Adonis.'

Today, the palace is still used for entertaining and state events, such as the 1992 Middle East Peace Conference, but most of the time it is open for visits (Monday to Saturday 9.30am–5pm, Sunday and holidays 9am–2pm; free Wednesday to EC citizens). It has its highlights – the clock collection, some grand 18th-century embroidery, porcelain and glass, Tiepolo's painted ceilings in the Throne Room – but be warned: you walk several kilometres inside, and it's not to every taste. There are also separate small museums in the old Pharmacy, Armoury and Library, and wonderful gardens with the carriages museum reached off the Paseo de la Virgen de Puerto (*see p. 87*). A good place to stop for a drink en route, though you cannot sit down, is **El Anciano Rey de Vinos** (Bailén, 19), which has its own sweet and dry wines.

In festival dress

A lighter nearby alternative to the exhausting Royal Palace is the little that remains of Arab Madrid. The unfinished 19th-century Catedral de la Almudena stands on top of the first walled Arab city, but if you take the Cuesta de la Vega immediately to the right, you come to the Parque de Emir Mohammed II (down to the left), where you can pick out square towers in a section of the **Arab wall**. The 9th-century sections are of large stones bound with adobe, and the 10th-century ones of masonry, plus later strips of brickwork. Opposite, a plaque marks the site of the Puerta de la Vega, the main entrance to the Arab town, next to which a replica of the Virgin de Almudena is installed where she was (mythically) discovered at the Reconquest.

Back at the top, walking on to the other side of the viaduct – a favourite suicide jump – Calle de la Morería, to the left, leads down into the **Plaza del Alamillo**, the centre of the Arab quarter after the Reconquest. You can then double back up Calle Alfonso VI, where the Christian conquerors entered the town and down Redondilla and Agustín Mancebo, strolling through lovely quiet thoroughfares whose hills and curves have hardly changed since medieval times.

From either here or the palace, head up the **Calle Mayor**. As you turn up, you pass on the right the 17th-century Palacio de Uceda built by the secretary of Philip III, the Duque de Uceda. Further

Recharge in Retiro Park

up, you pass the junction with Calle Traviesa in 1913 where Alfonso XIII and his new wife, Victoria Eugenia, Queen Victoria's favourite granddaughter, were nearly assassinated when a bomb was thrown down on their wedding carriage. As it was, the blood from a decapitated guard splashed through the open window and on to the wedding dress.

A photo of the bombing – and of bullfighters and various other historical incidents – hangs on the walls of **Casa Ciriaco** (Calle Mayor 84; Tel: 2480620), on the ground floor of the house from which the bomb was thrown. This is a good place to have lunch, with all sorts of traditional dishes such as chicken *pepitoria*, and a front bar for an *aperitivo*. If you feel like something more filling, double back to **La Bola** (Calle La Bola 5; Tel: 5476930) for *cocido*.

After lunch, you can either take the Metro to the **Retiro Park** (Sol to Retiro) or walk there (30 minutes) along the old royal route: the Calle Mayor, the east-west axis of the old town since Arab times, and Calle Alcalá, which takes you past the Academia de Bellas Artes de San Fernando and the Círculo de Bellas Artes (Calle Alcalá 42), a wonderful place for a coffee in *belle-époque* surroundings. On the diagonally opposite corner of Plaza de la Cibeles is the **Palacio de Linares** (Tuesday to Friday 9–11.30am, Saturday and Sunday 10am–12.30pm; fee), a splendid palace built by José de Murga (1872), one of few ennobled bourgeoisie of the 19th century. The interior – considered the most important of its period in Spain – has recently been restored at the cost of 600 million pesetas, and the ballroom, Chinese room, Byzantine chapel, murals and wooden ceilings are now open to the public (Paseo de Recoletos 2).

To reach the park from here, continue up to the **Puerta de Alcalá** (1779), designed as a grandiose royal gateway to the city. In the 1980s it took on a new life, commemorated in

Filling food in La Bola

a rock song, as a symbol of the city's new tolerance. Diagonally opposite is one of the main gateways into the Retiro Park, which takes its name from '*Buen Retiro*' or Good Retreat, the name given to the bosky Monastery of the Jerónimos after the court took to retiring there at Christmas and Lent. Finally, in 1632, Philip IV built a palace next to it, with huge gardens which opened to the public at the end of the 18th century, and, despite much damage in the War of Independence, became a park in 1868.

The main Avenida Méjico leads up to the boating lake, one of the few surviving elements from the old palace, which was used in royal times for fiestas and extravagant operettas (boating, 10am–sunset). On Sunday mornings and summer afternoons, the surrounding paths are alive with *Madrileños* walking their dogs or children, going for a romantic stroll, cruising or having a drink at the kiosks. Among them, you find fortune-tellers, joggers, street-theatre, and seasonal attractions; in June, for example, there is a book fair.

Most of the landscaping is now post-18th century: heading right and down from the lake, you come upon the Palacio de Velázquez (1883), built for a mining exhibition, and the romantic Palacio de Cristal (1887), originally a glass-house for exotic plants. Older *Madrileños* remember going skating on its lake in winter. Further

on, up the Paseo Julia Romero Torres, is the rose garden, stunning from April to June, and, at its western end, the Fallen Angel (1870s), said to be the world's first statue of the devil. If you take the Paseo del Equador back to the lake and go left at the Plaza de Honduras, you'll come to a gate which brings you out opposite

The Palacio de Cristal

Calle de la Academia. Taking it, you pass the Iglesia de los Jerónimos, a church with long royal connections, where King Juan Carlos took his oaths in 1975.

An alternative to the park – or an addition to it if you have the energy – is the **Museo Thyssen-Bornemisza** (Puerta del Prado 8; Tel: 3690151, Metro Banco de España/Atocha; Tuesday to Sunday 10am–7pm; guided tours Tuesday to Friday 10–11am), a stunning collection of 600 paintings and sculptures from the 13th century to the present day, rented to the Spanish government for 9½ years. It needs six hours to see the lot, but if you want to dip in, you can pick and choose. Start at the top for Old Masters; at the bottom for the museum's outstanding 20th-century section, from Soviet

Constructivism to Pop Art.
Afterwards have a drink under the splendid modernist stained-glass dome of the **Palace Hotel** (Plaza de las Cortes 7). It is opposite the Cortes, where an army colonel held the parliament at gunpoint on 23 February 1981.

From the Palace, it's a 10-minute walk up to dinner at **Lhardy's** (Calle de San Jerónimo 8; Tel: 5213385; Metro Sol), with its splendid 19th-century dining-rooms and classic cuisine (game, crayfish soup and so on). The evening can be continued in the same style at the **Palacio de Gaviria** (Calle Arenal 9, Metro Sol/Opera; Monday to Saturday 8am–3pm and 7pm–midnight), another *nouveau-riche*, 19th-century palace and grandly theatrical as a place to drink.

DAY 3

Metropolis of the Visual Arts

In 1992, Madrid finally realised its grand 18th-century dream of a salon of the arts – a cluster of museums and galleries close together down the city's main avenue. They give a sweeping overview from prehistory to post-modernism which even those who don't consider themselves art-lovers find breathtaking.

– Starting point: Metro Serrano or Colón. State museums are closed on Sunday afternoon and Monday, and the Centro Reina Sofia on Tuesday –

The small but dazzling **Museo Arqueológico Nacional** (Calle Serrano 13; Tuesday to Saturday 9.30am–8.30pm, Sunday and holidays 9.30am–2.30pm; allow 1½ hours for a leisurely visit; fee), where you start the day, is the most undersold of Madrid's museums. Its collection – none of the pieces comes from youthful Madrid – moves from a reproduction

Museo Arqueológico Nacional

of the Altamira cave paintings through Iberian stone-carvings (the famous Dama de Elche, 3rd–4th century BC), Roman frescoes and sculptures, the Visigothic crown jewels, post-Reconquest Muslim decorative arts, and Romanesque church sculpture. After seeing these, one looks at Picasso and Miró with different eyes.

From here, cut down Calle Jorge Juan by the Plaza de Colón to the **Paseo de Recoletos**, the city's main north-south avenue. Once a *cañada* – or sheep-track – running alongside a stream on the eastern limits of the city, today it is Madrid's human river, an artery for traffic and people. In this lower half, it is also a social boundary: on the Right Bank are the upmarket areas of Salamanca and Retiro; on the Left Bank you'll find the jumbled popular quarters of Centro, Chamberi, Huertas and Atocha. If you feel in need of a cup of coffee, stop off at **Café Gijón** (Puerta de Recoletos 21), Madrid's classic literary café, founded in 1888. Opposite is one of the grandest palaces, now a cream and white bank, built by the Marqués de Salamanca who was responsible for developing the quarter of the same name.

Keeping south, the fountain of Cibeles marks the start of the **Paseo del Prado**, laid out in the mid-18th century as an open-air salon where carriages could circulate around a pedestrian promenade and three fountains (1777–92) fed by the underground stream: at the northern end, Cibeles, goddess of earth, her sceptre and clef representing her rule over the seasons; to the south, Neptune, originally facing Cibeles (Plaza Cánovas del Castillo); and in the centre, Apollo, fire and air (Plaza de la Lealtad). Underlying the classical allegory were other references: at one level, to Charles III's encouragement of agriculture, the navy, arts and sciences; on the other, to the magical symbolism fashionable at court at that time.

To this promenade was added first a botanical garden (1781) and

Madrileño matron

then a grand neoclassical museum planned to combine a natural history collection, an academy of sciences, and a congress of scientists. It was Ferdinand VII who decided to house the royal collections of art here in 1818, and they first opened to the public as the Museo del Prado the following year.

As you walk down from Cibeles to the Prado, you will pass later grandiose additions built on ex-crown lands: the ornate Palacio de Correos (always hard to believe it is only a post office); the **Bolsa** or stock exchange (1884), fascinating to nip into for 10 minutes (Plaza de la Lealtad 1; 10am–2.30pm, free admission) for the ceilings and action on the floor; and, opposite, the Ritz, built after Alfonso XIII's wedding in 1906 revealed the city's lack of aristocratic accommodation. Its wing-collared staff are so strict on security that it's said to be the only place Yasser Arafat is happy to stay without bodyguards.

Velázquez at the Prado

At the next junction, you come to the **Museo del Prado**, though the main entrance is through the Puerta de Murillo at the far end (Tuesday to Saturday 9am–7pm, Sunday and holidays 9am–2pm). The northern entrance gives access to the rather less interesting 19th-century collection of the **Casón del Buen Retiro** (Calle Felipe IV 13; 9am–7pm).

The size, range and density of the Prado collection – 8,000 paintings in all, of which only a fifth are on show – is such that you need repeated visits to digest it in full. If you are dipping in for only a few hours, it's a good idea to decide what you want to see. On the one hand, the unique feature of the collection is its breadth, the Spanish monarchs having bought much less locally than the Medicis. Hanging here are some of the greatest works of Bosch, Dürer, Botticelli, Raphael, Titian, Rubens and Rembrandt – and the list could go on. If this is what interests you, buy the *Key to the Prado* by Manuela Mena and Consuelo Luca de Tena as you go in, to locate the works you want to find. At a more serious level, private guides are available at 3,500 pesetas an hour.

A second approach, especially rewarding when linked to the other museums, is to concentrate on the native Spanish school. This takes around 2 hours, starting with the 15th-century painters such as Juan de Juanes and Pedro Berruguete; moving on to the imported

Centro Reina Sofía houses Picasso's 'Guernica' in a new art collection

mysticism of El Greco (1541–1614); the 17th-century religious passion of Ribera (1591–1652), who worked mainly in Naples, and Zurbarán (1598–1664), from Seville; and finally, the work of the two masters whose work is inextricably bound up with Madrid in terms of patronage and what they painted: Velázquez (1599–1660), whose painting *Las Meninas* is considered by some to be the greatest work of Western art, and Goya (1746–1828), whose paintings track an extraordinary progression from light tapestry designs to black horror.

What is so remarkable about looking at these paintings together is what they share: harsh psychological realism, intense light and shade, a looming awareness of death, and – perhaps most striking of all – the faces and skies you see outside on the street. Small information sheets on Goya and Velázquez, with basic background facts about their work, are available for a few pesetas as you go round the galleries.

When you need a break, the cafeteria in the basement isn't bad, or you can get some fresh air in the **Botanical Gardens** (Plaza de Murillo 2; 10am–sunset; admission fee, children free), invitingly cool and shady in the summer. Your Prado ticket will allow you back in again (same day only) if you get it stamped. For a change of atmosphere at lunch, cross the Paseo and cut up the Plaza Platería Martínez to **El Caldero** on Calle Huertas (*see restaurants, p. 68*). Another option is to move straight on to the **Centro Reina Sofía** (*see below*), and stop awhile in the excellent café there.

Atocha Station's tropical garden

It is in the Reina Sofía, the new national 20th-century art collection, that the line of inheritance in Spanish painting is really brought home. Nicknamed the Sofidou because it aims to rival the Pompidou Centre in Paris, it is housed in an 18th-century hospital with flashy hi-tech glass lifts slapped on the front (Museo Nacional Centro de

Arte Reina Sofía, Calle Santa Isabel 2; Monday and Wednesday to Saturday 10am–9pm, Sunday 10am–2.30pm; allow 1½ hours). Here, one huge canvas stands out: Picasso's *Guernica*, painted in a 4-day fury in 1937 after the first deliberate wartime bombing of a civilian population, the Basque town of Guernica, on which incendiary bombs were dropped to burn houses on top of the victims.

The painting touches the centre of the Spanish psyche and its references to the past are unmissable: the all-seeing bull as the eternal Spain; the crucified soldier, reminiscent of Velázquez, crushed beneath the horse of Franco's military grip; the agonised faces of war, as Goya had depicted them. It touches a national nerve since Picasso would not allow it to be brought to Spain until the country was once again a republic. When it finally arrived in 1981, it went on show behind bullet-proof glass in an annexe to the Prado, then, in 1992, was moved here – again controversially, since Picasso had expressly wanted it hung near Velázquez's and Goya's work.

After such a visual binge, the tropical garden of the nearby late 19th-century iron and glass **Atocha Railway Station** (on the Plaza Emperador Carlos) is a great place to rest your feet in a semi-tropical atmosphere. If you need a stronger pick-me-up, aim straight for **Museo Chicote**, Gran Vía 12, Madrid's legendary cocktail bar. Stories about Chicote are legion, based both on owner Perico Chicote, who once knocked out a customer who was rude to a waiter's mother, and his clientele, which ranged from politicians and prostitutes to black-market dealers and birds of passage like Hemingway. 'Perico, if your bar's for whores, then I'm a whore,' Ava Gardner is supposed to have said. The prostitutes went when the bar was spruced up in 1981, but the service and cocktails haven't changed. After a couple of *mojitos criollos*, Hemingway's favourite of rum, lemon juice, mint, sugar and soda water, you'll be glad it's only a 5-minute walk round the corner to **Casa Salvador** (Calle Barbieri 12), a classic postwar *tasca*.

If your legs are still capable of working, a night-time stroll along **Gran Vía** makes a great contrast to a day of high culture. By night, neon, floodlights, and hand-painted cinema placards convert it into a garish small Broadway backdrop that *Madrileños* love to hate. You can happily spend a couple of hours people-watching in the pavement cafés, but try to make your drinks last as they're pricey.

The Gran Vía

Option 1. Convents and Churches

You need 3 to 4 hours to see this selection of Madrid's convents and churches. Plainer from the outside than within, they contain everything from medieval 'mudéjar' architecture to stunning baroque frescoes.

– Starting point: Metro Opera –

Until the early 19th century, Madrid was overwhelmingly a monastic and church city. The 18th-century playwright Ramón de la Cruz put these words into the mouth of one of his characters: 'The capital has more churches than homes, more priests than laymen, and more altars than kitchens; even in the entrances of the filthy houses, even in the vile taverns, small paper altarpieces can be seen, along with a medley of wax articles, small basins of holy water and religious lamps.' In part, such religiosity was the inheritance of the Inquisition. Perhaps more important, the religious orders owned an astonishing 75 percent of property in the city until the 19th century,

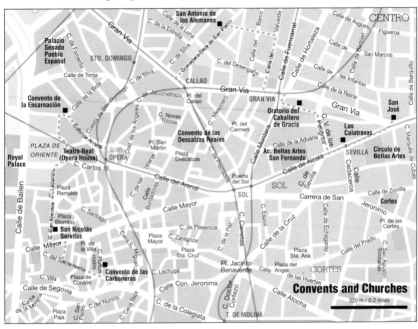

Convents and Churches

320 m / 0.2 miles

Peddling religion

when many of the convents and monasteries were pulled down. Today the *Madrileños* are not especially devout, but, even so, religion is a part of everyday life: the outsider's eye picks up on streets named after saints, fiestas marking religious feast days, crucifixes in shops and lobbies, nuns on the street, shops crammed with kitschy religious objects, and formal Easter processions.

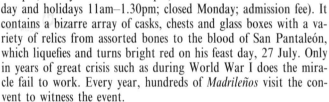

The Spanish also love relics. This tour starts at the royal **Convento de la Encarnación**, founded by Philip II's daughter-in-law, Queen Margaret of Austria, where there is an extraordinary reliquary room (Plaza de la Encarnación; Metro Opera; Tuesday to Thursday 10.30am–12.30pm and 4–5.30pm, Friday 10.30am–12.30pm, Sunday and holidays 11am–1.30pm; closed Monday; admission fee). It contains a bizarre array of casks, chests and glass boxes with a variety of relics from assorted bones to the blood of San Pantaleón, which liquefies and turns bright red on his feast day, 27 July. Only in years of great crisis such as during World War I does the miracle fail to work. Every year, hundreds of *Madrileños* visit the convent to witness the event.

A short walk across the Plaza de Oriente – where you can have a coffee in the Café de Oriente – and up Calle Lepanto, then down San Nicolás, is the church of **San Nicolás Servitas**, the only one of Madrid's original 13 medieval parish churches still intact (9am–1.30pm and 5.30–8.30pm, ring the bell in Travesia del Biombo 1, if the door isn't open). It has clear *mudéjar* traces: notably, a fine brick tower – possibly the minaret of an earlier mosque – with a triple layer of blind Moorish arches on ceramic columns; a horseshoe arch; and plasterwork decoration. In one of the side-chapels is an interesting exhibition of medieval Madrid.

Crossing to the other side of Calle Mayor, then right down Calle Traviesa, along Calle del Sacramento and left up the narrow Calle Puñonrostro, is the Plaza del Conde de Miranda, where the nuns of the **Convento de las Carboneras** (10am–1pm and 4–7pm; walk straight across, through the church or, if it is closed, ring at No 3) – so called because the image of the Virgin was found in a coalyard – sell delicious small cakes and biscuits, such as *mantecados de jerez* (sherry biscuits). The church itself, which you can also visit,

San Nicolás Servitas

keeps a 17th-century altarpiece, sculpture and paintings. Opposite the convent is a palace renowned in the 19th century for selling miraculous Bibles made with the skin of dead children. Five minutes' walk away, at Calle Toledo 43, you can buy tall white church candles.

If you are interested in architecture, you may like to see a trio of baroque churches built during the building splurge that attended the arrival of the court. Within 10 minutes' walk of each other, they can be visited in succession in the late morning. **San Antonio de los Alemanes** (Corredera Baja de San Pablo 16; Metro Callao; 9am–1pm), founded as a hospital for the Portuguese at court in 1624, is covered with 800 sq m (8,600 sq ft) of stunning frescoes by Giordano, Coello and de Ricci. A quarter of an hour's walk away is **Las Calatravas**, built 1686–88, (Calle Alcalá 25; 11.30am–noon and 12.30pm–1pm), with its altarpiece encrusted with garlands, designed and built for the then fabulous sum of 80,000 ducados by José Churriguera. Five minutes down the road from here is San José, built between 1730 and 1742 (Calle Alcalá 43; noon–12.30pm and 1–1.30pm), with an array of polychrome (coloured wood) sculpture, a unique Spanish genre.

A bleeding Christ in San José

The route also takes you past the city's finest neoclassical church, the **Oratorio de Caballero de Gracia**, built 1790–95, (10am–2pm and 5–9pm). Designed by Juan de Villanueva, the 'architect of shadows' and of the Prado, its Corinthian columns are thought to have masonic symbolism. Over the altar hangs the Cristo de la Agonía, a baroque masterwork, while round the back on Gran Vía – which was specially re-routed in order to accommodate the building – it has a bold new post-modernist facade of concrete, marble and glass.

Option 2. The Craft Tradition

A full morning devoted to the city's range of old and new crafts, taking in the Museum of Decorative Arts and a selection of specialist shops.

– Starting point: Metro Banco de España/Retiro –

Even if you do not go in search of Madrid's craft tradition, you will stumble upon it all over the city: *barquilleros* selling wafer cones in the park in summer; *castañeras* with chestnut-roasting barrels in winter; knife-sharpeners, who play whistles to announce their arrival by motorbike; barbers who give double shaves designed to last several days; *zapateros* (shoe menders) repairing rips and tears that seem impossible to mend. All approach their trade as if it were a craft. At window No 86 in the central post office, your parcels are carefully wrapped with brown paper, string and hot sealing-wax.

To appreciate the history of the Spanish craft tradition, first spend an hour in the small **Museo de Artes Decorativas** (Calle Montalbán 12; Monday to Friday 9am–3pm, Saturday and Sunday 10am–2pm; allow 1 hour; fee), where ceramics, wood, textiles and industrial arts, plus a life-size Valencian kitchen, show off their strength as everyday decorative arts.

Traditionally, Madrid's craft workshops were clumped in the quarter of old Madrid around the Puerta Cerrada, where muleteers and wagon-drivers came from every region to sell their wares and buy tools and supplies such as bellows, sieves and ropes. It's also here, especially around **Cava Baja** (Metro Latina) that the main vestiges of those traditions survive.

If you arrive by 10.30am, have a late breakfast of *churros*, sugary fritters, at the **Fábrica de Churros** (Cava Baja 7) and watch them being fried in great Catherine-wheels. Almost opposite, at No 12, is José

A guitar-maker's window

Muñóz, a barrel-maker who makes casks and work buckets in oak and chestnut, mainly on commission, although some in the shop are for sale. Next door, at No 10, is the wood-turners' studio where Manuel Lopez's family have been making sieves, muzzles, darning eggs, mortars, bellows, mousetraps and fly-swats since 1926.

Further down the street, past specialist shops – such as Atanasio Garcia, at No 25, who sells every conceivable type of string and Salinero, at No 34, with ceramics and kitchen hardware – is José Goya, a guitar-maker, at No 42. The wood for the guitars is palosanto, imported from Brazil for the body and hoops, ebony

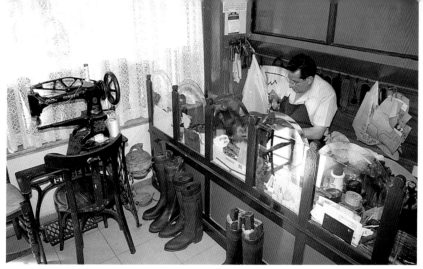

Zapatería Tenorio: shoe-maker of distinction

brought from Gabón for the fingerboard, spruce pine from Germany for the cover, and cedar and cypress from Aranjuez for the handle. They also sell picks and strings.

Nearby at Calle Toledo 43, the smell of warm wax exudes from Victor Ortega, one of the last remaining *cererías*, or candle-makers. Their main trade is still in the long white candles for churches – not expensive – but you can also buy smaller, more decorative ones (the candles are made in the morning only). At Zapatería Tenorio (Plaza de la Provincia 6, Tel: 2664440), beautiful (but not cheap) handmade country boots and shoes are made; they are used to taking measurements and orders and sending the finished shoes by post. All these workshops are open 9.30am–1.30pm.

If you have a special interest in crafts not satisfied by this itinerary then visit the **Fundación de Gremios** (Polígono Industrial Fuencarral, Calle Labastida 10–12; Metro Begona; 10.30am–1.30pm; fee), a complex of workshops where you can find porcelain, furniture and textiles being made.

Option 3. El Capricho de Alameda de Osuna

A visit to the 18th-century garden at Alameda (minimum 2 hours) and, for those with a car, on to the historic town of Alcalá de Henares where Cervantes was born (another 2 hours). You may like to take a drink or picnic to the garden; nothing is on sale nearby.

– To the garden: Metro to Canillejas and a short walk, or by car along NII (beware of traffic jams) and taking exit and signs for Barajas pueblo –

In 1797, the Duchess of Osuna, friend of Goya and arch-rival of the Duchess of Alba, managed to lure Marie-Antoinette's gardener, Jean-Baptiste Mulot, to Madrid, to transform the bare fields on the road to Alcalá de Henares into a Romantic landscape garden. He used the ample water supply from wells to build an artificial river, lake, fountains, and grottoes, creating what Victorian traveller and diarist Lady Holland described in 1803 as 'gardens contrived for coolness'. It later came to be known as El Capricho.

A restoration programme is nearing completion and the garden (Saturday, Sunday and holidays 9am–8pm, or sunset if earlier) has never looked lovelier. In spring, when the expanse of lilac is a sea of fragrant colour, it's spectacular.

Lady Holland also commented on 'innumerable grottoes, temples, chaumières, hermitages, excavations, canals, ports, pleasure boats, islands...' Over the next 50 years, with a brief break during the War of Independence, the Duchess continued the work, hiring Spanish set designer Angél María Tadey to build picturesque architectural features, adding a maze and planting a huge variety of trees. After her death, the garden slowly decayed; the last of the line, Duke Mariano, ruined himself with a series of outlandish extravagances and left so many debts that the garden had to be auctioned in 1896. Finally, it served as an army headquarters in the Civil War and a huge bunker was built underneath. Only in 1974 was the garden salvaged by the town council, and the painstaking work of restoration begun.

A good approach from the main gates is circular, starting up to the left past the **Old Woman's House**, a beamed cottage with *trompe l'oeil* paintings inside; continuing up to the octagonal **Dance Casino** with its allegorical ceilings, lake and boathouse in the

Garden masonry

upper English garden; then passing along the artificial river to the model fort, and down through the middle or French garden, to the lilac maze, the **Exedra**, and other various architectural features constructed in the 1790s.

If you go by car, it's only 20 minutes up the NII motorway to **Alcalá de Henares** (by train or bus, you cannot make the link, but trains go direct from Madrid to Alcalá every 15 minutes, taking half an hour; and buses leave from Avenida de América 34, every 15 minutes and take 40 minutes). Birthplace of Miguel de Cervantes, author of *Don Quixote*, it has a fine historic centre despite industrial outskirts. The **Archbishop's Palace** (1537) and **University facade**

El Capricho de Alameda de Osuna

(1537–53) are highlights of the Spanish Renaissance; the **Casa-Museo Cervantes** (Calle Mayor; Monday to Friday 10am–2pm and 4–7pm; allow 30 minutes), where the writer was born, can be visited; and there are numerous convents, monasteries and churches off the arcaded high street. Of the various old taverns, the **Hostería de Estudiantes** (Calle Colegios 3; Tel: 888 0330), part of the Parador system, is a beautiful Renaissance building; it serves thick hot chocolate and other Castilian snacks to put you back on your feet – or, if you want to stay for the evening, a Cervantine dinner served by costumed waiting staff.

Option 4. San Antonio de la Florida

Madrid's River Manzanares leads you down to the hermitage nicknamed 'the Sistine Chapel of Spanish impressionism' on account of its Goya frescoes. Allow 4 hours for this, walking back to the city through the Parque del Oeste.

– Starting point: Metro Norte –

The shady riverside terrace starts just below the Estación del Norte, a florid 19th-century railway station (Metro Norte, from Opera). To get to it descend the steps off Paseo de la Florida just opposite the station. In the 1970s this stretch was reclaimed and the duck houses were built by Tierno Galván, Madrid's charismatic mayor. A short stroll takes you down to the Puente de Reina Victoria and the Glorieta de la Florida, where there are cafés (the Florida does good *tapas*) and the hermitage of **San Antonio de la Florida**.

Goya's frescoes

In fact, there are two twin hermitages. The one on the left is a replica, built in 1905 so that Goya's frescoes would be better protected. The original (Monday to Friday 9am–2pm; free admission on Wednesday) was built from 1792. Goya, recognised as the greatest painter of his day through his court paintings, was given a free hand to decorate it. He completed the work in only 4 months, transferring the outlines of sketches on paper into the wet plaster with a knife, painting rapidly on to the wet plaster and then dry-painting on top.

Temple of Debod

At the time of painting these frescoes Goya was recovering from an illness which left him deaf and sardonically critical of frivolous aristocratic Madrid. They show the beginning of a freer, impressionistic style filled with witty and incisive social detail.

The frescoes illustrating the miracle of San Antonio of Lisbon raising a man from the dead broke with the convention of depicting heavenly beings and instead portrayed the people of Madrid: cherubims like street-kids and curvy female angels watch over figures picked straight out of Madrid society. Since 1989, the frescoes have been undergoing restoration to repair the damage done by fire and water during the Civil War, and the rich tones of the colours – ochres, blues and browns – have returned. The work will be completed in 1994.

Under the frescoes is Goya's tomb, erected in 1919 when his body was brought back from Bordeaux, where he died. The skeleton inside is headless, since a Spanish doctor, curious to know what the brain of a genius was like, plundered the tomb in Bordeaux.

Next to the hermitage is **Casa Mingo**, Paseo de la Florida 2 (10am–8pm), an excellent Asturian tavern, cheap and cheerful, where you can eat delicious spit-roast chicken and blue goat's cheese, drink cider and sit outside in the summer. It is packed at

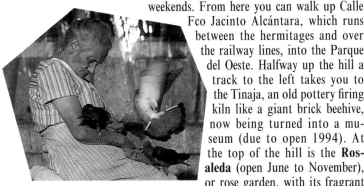

Birds in the hand

weekends. From here you can walk up Calle Fco Jacinto Alcántara, which runs between the hermitages and over the railway lines, into the Parque del Oeste. Halfway up the hill a track to the left takes you to the Tinaja, an old pottery firing kiln like a giant brick beehive, now being turned into a museum (due to open 1994). At the top of the hill is the **Rosaleda** (open June to November), or rose garden, with its fragrant blocks of colour. Further up the stepped path (to the right of the rose garden as you come out of it), you emerge at Paseo de Pintor Rosales, where you can have a drink at the *terrazas*, or wander along to the nearby **Templo de Debod**, an ancient Egyptian temple. This is a good place to see sunsets.

To return, the closest Metro is then Ventura Rodriguez. Alternatively you can pick up the **Teleférico**, or cable car, at the Balcón de Rosales, which takes you down to the Casa de Campo park.

Monument to a passion

Option 5. Bullfighting Madrid

Allow 2 hours to visit the bullring and its museum, plus the favourite aficionados' bar, then come back to town to see matadors' suits being made.

– Take the Metro to Las Ventas –

'Nothing,' wrote Jan Morris, 'expresses the mescalin quality of this country better than the bullfight, that lurid and often tawdry gladiatorial ritual, which generally repels the northerner in theory, but often makes his blood race in the act.'

Madrid is one of the world capitals of bullfighting and, even if you would never want to sit through a fight, it is fascinating to glimpse its history and ritual through Spanish eyes at the **Museo Taurino**, or Museum of Bullfighting. In addition, the huge **Plaza de Toros** (Calle Alcalá 231), which holds over 23,000 people and is the second largest bullring in the world after Mexico City is a monument in its own right, nicknamed 'the cathedral of bullfighting'.

Built in 1929 in brick neo-*mudéjar* style, the ring is decorated with shields of famous bullrings around the outside. Round the back of the ring, to the right, is the Patio de Caballos – the horses' courtyard – and the Museo Taurino (Tuesday to Friday and Sunday 9.30am–2.30pm; admission free). The museum, labelled in English and Spanish, doesn't go into the origins of bullfighting (thought to lie in Iberian wedding rituals), but it includes plenty of surprises, such as the 16th-century papal bull laying down excommunication for pro-bullfighting monarchs, and a suit which belonged to Juanita Cruz, the greatest woman bullfighter. There are also paintings and engravings showing the early bullfights in the Plaza Mayor and the 18th-century bullring next to the Puerta de Alcalá, plus the obligatory bulls' heads and heroic portraits of the most famous bullfighters.

In the patio opposite the museum is the **Sala de Prensa**, which prints the posters advertising fights. If you go during the season (and sometimes, if you're lucky, out of it), they'll give you one or two recent ones. After your visit, have a drink at **Los Timbales**, Calle Alcalá 227 (7am–1am), one of the traditional bars for aficionados. It is named after the drums used in the opening ceremony of the bullfight, which are kept here.

The only way you can see inside the ring is by going to one of the sporadic rock concerts held here, or a bullfight itself. The season reaches a climax in the 20-day Feria de San Isidro, the world's most important season, starting in the second week of May, when there are also a couple of the horseback *corridas* (*de rejones*). There's a central ticket office (Calle La Victoria 9; Metro Sol), with

Many bars are shrines to the art of bullfighting

prices from 900–11,000pesetas for the best seats, in the shade, but they're hard to lay your hands on without recourse to touts. If you do get a ticket, go in *madrileño* spirit with a hip-flask and keep an ear open to the crowd's famously critical banter, then read the write-up on the arts pages of *El País* the following day.

If you don't get a ticket, you can still go to the **Venta del Batán** in the Casa del Campo (Metro Batán), where the the bulls are kept in pens on the day before a fight. From October to May, it is also the venue for the municipal bullfighting school (late afternoon) where young *novilleros* train with capes and straw bulls.

Back in town, you may like to get a closer look at the tailors who make the bullfighters' suits and even, if you have a spare £5,000, have a suit made. **Sastrería Justo Algaba**, Calle de la Paz 4 (Metro Sol) and **Angela Gonzalez López**, Plaza General Vera del Rey 11 (Metro Latina), are two of the best.

Option 6. Sunday Morning at the Rastro

A trip to the Rastro street-market can be combined with an 'aperitivo' in Lavapiés – the most lively of the old Madrid quarters – and a visit to the Puerta de Toledo shopping market. Allow at least 3 hours.

– Starting point: La Latina –

Sunday mornings in Madrid usually mean a long lie-in, a trip to the country or a visit to the **Rastro flea-market**, a sprawling hive of stalls and shops with everything from caged birds to snails, books, crafts and clothes. It runs down from the **Plaza del Cascorro**, named after a battle in Cuba in 1901 at which a Lavapiés orphan, Eloy Gonzalo, heroically set fire to the walls. A statue depicts

Bargain-hunters

Sunday morning at the Rastro

him with the rope he attached to himself, so that his fellows could pull back his body if he died.

From here, the market runs down the **Ribera de Curtidores**, and up the side streets, especially the Plaza del General Vara del Rey. Bargaining is the norm on second-hand items (this is often said to be the most African or Arab of the European markets); start a third lower than the price offered and go up from that. Articles for sale tend to be grouped by type. Antiques, for example, are in the Plaza del Rey, Plaza Campillo and the building of the old *rastro* (slaughterhouse), below the Calle del Carnero, after which it is thought the market is named.

When you have had enough of the market and the street-music – watch out for the gypsy group with a goat and Algerian *rai* (a distinct Arab rock) – you can have a look round **Lavapies**, named after a fountain for washing feet at the bottom of the quarter. In the 15th century, this was the old *judería* (Jewish quarter), which has left its mark in higgledy-piggledy streets, the remains of a synagogue under the church of San Lorenzo and the Catholic street names given when the Jews were expelled. Known for its street culture, this has been the birthplace of many bullfighters and much colourful slang.

Take the Calle de San Cayetano (the first left as you go down Ribera de Curtidores), where paintings are sold. At the end, in Calle de Embajadores, is the **Iglesia de San Cayetano** – patron saint of births – its facade by Churriguera and Ribera. On his feast day, 7 August, the saint's image is covered with flowers and paraded around the streets; if you manage to pull off a flower, tradition has it that bread and work are guaranteed for a year. Going on down Embajadores to Calle Sombrerete and the ruins of Sta Catalina, you

In the atmospheric Lavapiés

come to one of the *corrales*, the tall balconied buildings used as popular theatres from the 17th century.

If your stomach is rumbling by now, there are various options: the **Oso y Madroño** bakery (Calle Caravaca 10) for vegetable and fruit pies; the **Taberna de Antonio Sanchez** (Calle Mesón de Paredes 13), a bar with bullfighting and artistic associations, with good *tapas*; **Nuevo Café Barbieri** (Plaza Lavapiés), one of the oldest bars in town; or **Los Caracoles** (Plaza del Cascorro 18), for snails and seafood. They're all packed on Sunday lunchtime, but that's part of the attraction. If you feel like going to a restaurant, aim for **Malacatín**, (Calle Ruda 5, Tel: 2655241), which serves great *cocido*, rabbit and Valdepeñas wines.

Also open on a Sunday, and very close to the Rastro down the Calle Mira el Sol, off to the right on the bottom of Ribera de Curtidores, is the **Puerta de Toledo** (Sunday 10.30am–2.30pm, Tuesday to Saturday 10.30am–9pm), a fish-market converted into a fashion, craft, antique and design centre in the 1980s.

Option 7. High-rise Madrid

A bus ride and walk up the Paseo de Castellana, where high-rise blocks sprout among 19th-century palaces, is something you can do at any time of day. Allow 2 to 3 hours, plus time for a high-rise drink.

– Starting point: Metro Colón –

The **Paseo de Castellana**, built in the last two centuries as a northerly extension from the Paseo del Prado, has always been a corridor of power. In the 19th century, the tone was set by aristocratic palaces, but today it is dominated by modern banks and office blocks whose value goes up to 600,000pesetas a square metre.

A good starting point is the massive waterfall of the **Plaza Colón**. From underneath, it converts into a roaring wave, brilliantly evoking Columbus's journey in 1492. Above, skateboarders dodge around a 19th-century statue of Columbus and abstract boat-like sculptures (1977) by Vaquéros Turcos.

The Torre de Picasso

Walking north on the same side of the Castellana, you come after six short blocks to the open-air museum of sculpture, curiously tucked under the Eduardo Dato/Juan Bravo flyover. A motley collection, it includes *El Encuentro* ('The Meeting'), six tons of cement suspended on iron cords, by Basque sculptor Eduardo Chillida.

49

From here you can take a No 5, 150 or 27 (circular) bus up the Castellana, to the **Plaza de Castilla**. Among the most striking buildings are, on your left, No 32, a truncated pyramid of offices (1979), on your right, at Plaza San Juan de la Cruz, the Museo de Ciencias Naturales, then immediately on your left again, the cold

Down the Castellana

grey government buildings of the 1930s Nuevos Ministerios and the 1960s high-rise complex of AZCA, which ends at the Palacio de Congresos, with a mosaic frieze by Miró (1980). Opposite is the huge Estadio Santiago Bernabeu, home of football-club Real Atlético.

Another half-dozen stops take you to the Plaza itself, rechristened the Puerta de Europa since acquiring two dramatically slanting glass-faced blocks, called the **Torres Kio** (1992), as a northern gateway into the city.

Returning down the other side of the Paseo on the bus – you pay again even if it's the circular No 27 – get off again at AZCA, just after the Congress Hall. One of Madrid's main financial centres, covering 204 hectares (504 acres), it was designed along the lines of 1960s American architecture. The most interesting of its buildings is the tall BBV, No 79–80 (1974–80), built in ochre-coloured aluminium which gradually changes colour as it rusts with age. Designed by Saenz de Oiza, one of Spain's leading modern architects, its foundations are a giant 100-m (330-ft) arch built over the Metro line running underneath. The basement art gallery puts on excellent shows.

The stairs up to the right behind the BBV building take you into paved **gardens** with trees and fountains. From here you see the Alfredo Mau building, a curving wave of glass; the white metallic Torre de Picasso by Minoru Yamasaki, 150m (490ft) high, with 46 floors and five basements; and the Torre Europa, a round tower 31 storeys high, with a heliport surrounded by iron spikes nicknamed the 'crown of thorns'. On the 29th floor is **Club 95**, a pricey restaurant where you can have a pricey gourmet meal and a splendid view over the Castellana (Tel: 5568261; 1–4pm and 9–12pm).

A cheaper alternative a Metro or taxi ride away is the 32nd-floor **Casa de Cantabria** (Plaza de España 18; Metro Plaza de España; 9am–9pm), which charges just 100pesetas for access to a wonderful viewing balcony. It has a friendly bar serving simple lunches.

EXCURSIONS

Excursion 1. El Escorial

Allow at least 4 hours to visit El Escorial, Philip II's palace. Returning via Franco's Monument to the Fallen takes 2 hours, or a longer route through wonderful countryside past one of the best preserved Roman roads in the world another 5 hours.

– To El Escorial: by train (from Atocha, every half hour, journey time 1 hour), or by car along the NVI, taking the El Escorial exit (C505) –

When Philip II decided in 1563 to build a royal pantheon, with a monastery and summer palace attached, his brief to architect Juan de Herrera ran: 'Above all, do not forget what I have told you – simplicity of form, severity in the whole, nobility without arrogance, majesty without ostentation.'

Whether he achieved this at **El Escorial** (Tuesday to Sunday 10am–7pm, closed Monday; guided groups 10am–12.45pm and 4–7pm, 45 minutes), 56km (35 miles) from Madrid, in the foothills of the Sierra de Guadarrama northwest of Madrid, is a moot point. Representing an extreme search for academic truth, stripped clear of all ornament, the palace has always divided opinion.

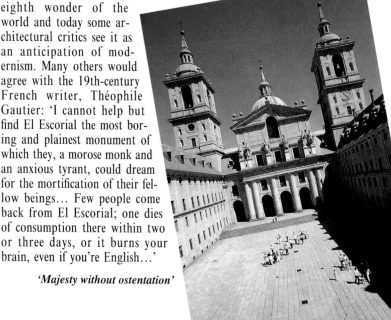

When it was built, it was called the eighth wonder of the world and today some architectural critics see it as an anticipation of modernism. Many others would agree with the 19th-century French writer, Théophile Gautier: 'I cannot help but find El Escorial the most boring and plainest monument of which they, a morose monk and an anxious tyrant, could dream for the mortification of their fellow beings... Few people come back from El Escorial; one dies of consumption there within two or three days, or it burns your brain, even if you're English...'

'Majesty without ostentation'

Undeniably, though, it is the essence of Spanish history: here, among other things, are the octagonal marble **Pantheon** of its monarchs (and their mothers); the offices where Philip boasted he ruled the world from two inches of paper, and one of the greatest libraries in the West – although today you may see only reproductions. Its scale is also the most forceful expression of the Spanish urge to absolutism: the giant parallelogram, with twin bell-towers of over 70m (230ft), has 15 cloisters, 16 patios, 88 fountains, 86 stairs, 1,200 doors and 2,600 windows.

It also adds to a visit if you understand the religious symbolism employed at El Escorial. The site was picked as a meeting point of sky and earth, its northwesterly direction from Madrid symbolic of a meeting with God. Equally, the outer courtyards were built in a grid shape to commemorate Spain's victory in 1557 at St Quentin on the feast day of St Lawrence, who was burnt on a griddle (he is said to have turned over when done on one side).

If you go by car, you can take a detour via **Valdemorillo** (take the El Pardillo turn-off from the C505, then the C600), a sierra village which has kept its character and some good bars, and arrive at El Escorial on the road by the **Silla de Felipe** (King Philip's Seat), high rocks with an impressive view of the palace, from where Philip II is said to have watched the building works in progress.

There is easy parking in town, by the palace itself, the contents of which need 2½ hours to see. If you are not going round with a guide, it would be worthwhile reading a guidebook beforehand. If

you don't want to go in, you can see the main patios and church without a ticket, and get a feeling of the classical strictness which influences Spanish architecture to the present day.

After coming out into the intense light, you can recover in the **Jardín de Frailes** (10am–7pm), the monks' garden beyond the columns on the western side of the palace, and/or in one of two

Reading up in El Escorial

restaurants: **Charoles**, Calle Floridablanca 24 (Tel: 8905975), excellent, but pricey, traditional and *nueva cocina* cooking – or, more cheaply, in **La Cueva**, Calle San Antón 4 (Tel: 8901516).

Now a polite, small town where middle-class families go for the summer, El Escorial has little else to see except annexes to the main palace, such as the 18th-century **Casita de Arriba**, about 1km (½ mile) out of town beyond the western front.

The direct route (C600) back to Madrid via the motorway takes you past **Santa Cruz del Valle de los Caídos** (Tuesday to Sunday 10am–6pm, closed Monday), or the Valley of the Fallen, the memorial built to those who died in the Civil War by Franco. A chilling

Memorial to the Fallen

parallel to El Escorial, it is a another cold exercise in scale – the basilica is carved into the rock under a 150-m (490-ft) high cross – with a tank included in the dome mosaic. Many Spaniards today resent it as a monument to Franco's dictatorship, and I would not personally recommend it, but some people admire it as a one-off feat of engineering.

A marvellous longer alternative by car takes you westwards via Robleda de Chavela (leave El Escorial on the C505 and turn off where marked) and Cebreros, a small wine town, to the **Puerto del Pico** pass (via the N403, C500 and C502). After driving through wonderful valleys of different landscape, you reach the Puerto (after 2 hours), one of the best preserved Roman roads in the world. Below it is the small town of **Mombeltrán** with its medieval castle, a pleasant place to stop for a drink. Signposted off the same road 5km (3miles) further on are the **Toros de Guisando**, Iberian stone bulls (who have lost their horns somewhere along the way). To return to Madrid, continue 30km (19 miles) down the C502 and pick up the NV motorway.

Excursion 2. Segovia and La Granja

You need at least 3 to 4 hours to stroll around Segovia city and visit a few of the sights; after lunch, allow 2 hours for the gardens of La Granja and 3 hours if you include a visit to the tapestry museum. Segovia is always 5–10°C (10–20°F) cooler than Madrid, so you may need to take a warm cover-up.

– It is 2 hours by train to Segovia (irregular departures from Chamartin), 1 hour by bus (Estación del Sur), or 1¼ hours by car, taking the NVI –

Of all the Castilian cities, **Segovia** most easily captures the imagination. Reminiscent of an Italian hill-town, it soars over the plains below: at its prow rises the an-

The fairy-tale Alcázar

Segovia's cathedral

gular wall of its turreted castle, at its masthead are the spires of its honey-stoned cathedral and churches, across its stern strides the great Roman aqueduct.

Less darkly historical than El Escorial or Toledo, it makes for a relaxing day out of Madrid. An accessible small town, it has kept characterful shops, great restaurants – wood-roast lamb and suckling pig are the real reason for many *Madrileños* coming here – and green countryside running up to the medieval wall. Inside there is much to see. This was a wealthy court city of the Middle Ages – Isabel of Castile was proclaimed queen here in 1474 – and it remains a vibrant cultural centre.

By car, after passing the Arab watch-tower at Torrelodones, then El Escorial and the Valle de los Caidos off to your left, you pass through the long Guadarrama tunnel built with Republican prisoner-of-war labour. Take the N603 turn-off and, as you run into Segovia, the N110 for Avila. From the aqueduct, the small road marked for La Fuencisla curves round the medieval town wall. Follow the sign to the Alcázar, a good place to park.

Local worker

From here, everything is within easy reach. Both the dramatically sited **Alcázar** (10am–7pm) and the **Cathedral** in the centre of town (9.30am–2pm and 3–6pm) are Late Gothic, combining a fairy-tale grace with earlier medieval severities softened by high-pitched turrets and parapets or filigree spires in the case of the cathedral. Both are more rewarding from the outside than the inside, though the cathedral has a serene elegance. Close to the cathedral, at Plaza Mayor No 10, is the tourist office where you can pick up a map.

It is worth trying to get access to a few of the two dozen 12th- and 13th-century Romanesque churches, characterised by Islamic architectural features, tiered bell-towers, arcaded stone galleries where the guilds used to meet, and carved capitals. In the old centre, **San Millán**, **San Martín** and **Santíssima Trinidad** are outstanding inside as well as out; these (and others) are open 11am–2pm during the summer season (otherwise, check the changing hours of Mass at the tourist office).

But to enjoy Segovia it isn't really necessary to visit anything. Much of its attraction is in small corners and quirky details discovered as you move around: the arches in Calle Velarde up from the Alcázar; the decorated *seraglio* plasterwork, *mudéjar* brickwork, and tiled street names; the small shops selling embroidery, leather goods and cakes. At the **Convento de las Dominicanas** (Calle Capuchino Alta 2; 9am–1pm, 4–6.30pm), you can buy small resin religious figures – mainly angels and saints, such as black Fray Escobar, which are hand-made by the nuns. In Calle Licenciado Peralta 3, there's a wonderful candle workshop, **La Fabril Cerera** (10am–2pm and 5–8pm).

This same street will bring you to the lookouts over the **Aqueduct**. Built by the Romans around the turn of the 1st century AD to serve their fortress here, it was originally 14km (8¾ miles) long. The unbound blocks of granite have survived largely because the aqueduct supplied the town's water up until the 1960s. But in 1992, the alarm went up that pollution, bird droppings, cars and botched restoration had left the double-arched section close to collapse. Sections of the aqueduct are likely to be under wraps for years to come.

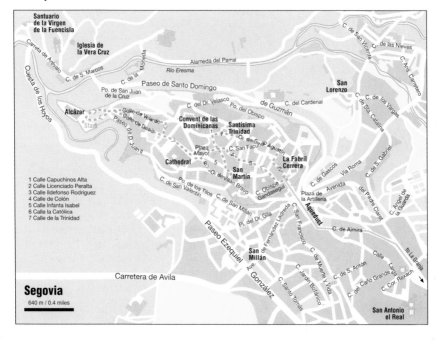

Before a late Spanish lunch, you might like to loop the walls. The one-way system leads down and out from the Alcázar on to the Cuesta de los Hoyos (turn right, as for Arévalo), and round under the town's prow to the **Fuencisla sanctuary**, which houses one of those curious Spanish Virgins with a military rank, in this case field-marshal. She was honoured in 1942 in thanks for saving the town from destruction in the Civil War. Up the next turning (for Zamarramala) is the wonderful **Iglesia de la Vera Cruz** (11am–2pm), a 12-sided, round-naved Templar church left to shepherds and gypsies for over a century until the Order of St John of Malta took it on in the 1950s. In the inner, top temple is the altar where aspiring knights had to keep a night's vigil watching over their arms. There are great views from the tower.

Continuing round in the same direction, you pass the huge, semi-ruined Santa Cruz church, and fork left down to the villagey quarter of **San Lorenzo**. The Romanesque church sits in a lovely 17th-century *mudéjar* brickwork, plaster and beamed *plaza*, painted ochre and sienna, with the odd shop, café and bar – good for an *aperitivo* and a sense of local life.

Wood-roasted lamb, suckling pig and frogs' legs are almost obligatory in Segovia's restaurants. The classic place to eat them is Mesón de Cándido, under the aqueduct (Calle Azoguejo 5, Tel: 428102; 12.30–4.40pm and 8–11.30pm). The historic setting and food justify the prices. Cheaper alternatives abound: for example, the Cueva de San Esteban, behind the Plaza Mayor (Calle Valdeáguila 15; Tel: 437811; 11.30am–1am; no credit cards).

After lunch take the road (N601) or bus (from the bus-station, Calle Ezequiel Gonzáles, 200m (650ft) from the aqueduct; leaves 1.30pm, 2pm, 3.15pm, and takes 15 minutes) to **San Ildefonso de la Granja**. As you leave Segovia, you pass the monastery of **San Antonio el Real** (4–7pm, ring the bell) on the right. It has several magnificent *artesanados* – *mudéjar* wooden ceilings – and a superbly detailed Flemish Calvary.

After some 15 minutes La Granja's elegant slate rooftops appear at the foot of the mountains. Here, Philip V, who had grown up at Versailles, nostalgically built a French-style summer palace (1719–39). More exciting than the ornate interior are the **water gardens** (summer 10am–9pm; winter till sunset) stretching up through sloping wood-

Strolling in the grounds of La Granja

land behind. The stunning gravity-fed fountains and waterfalls surpass those of many Italian Renaissance gardens, with ornate marble statuary scattered along paths through elm and chestnut woods graduating to majestic pines encircling a lake. The fountains, some of the highest in Europe, are switched on 3 days a week in late spring and early summer (check with the tourist office, as it depends on the winter's rainfall), but even without them the garden is extraordinarily beautiful.

Marble statuary abounds

What is interesting inside the palace is the **Tapestry Museum** (Tuesday to Friday 10am–1.30pm and 3–5pm; Sunday and holidays 10am–2pm), containing one of the best collections of medieval Flemish tapestries in Europe.

La Granja is famous for two other things – its glass factory, whose products you can find in gift-shops on the palace avenue or at the 18th-century factory itself, converted into a museum (Fundación Nacional Central de Vidrio), and its haricot beans, *judiónes de la Granja*, buttery-soft because of the soil and water. You can buy them in grocer's or eat them for supper, for example at **El Dollar** (Calle Valencia 1; Tel: 470269; 1.30–4pm and 9.30–11pm).

For a scenic return to Madrid, particularly enchanting on a late summer evening, take the road through pine forests over the Puerto de Navacerrada, the highest pass into Madrid (1,850m/6,000ft).

A second day can combine **Pedraza**, a perfect (if heavily restored) walled medieval village lying off the N110 north of Segovia; **Sepúlveda** – its Romanesque architecture two centuries earlier than Segovia's – sitting on a spur between two river valleys; and, from there, the spectacular **Hoces de Durantón**, a gorge frequented by eagles, with a dam and the small hermitage of San Frutos, all now protected as a natural park. You can then cut across country roads (13km/8 miles) to rejoin the NI at Cerezo de Abajo, 98km (61 miles) from Madrid.

Toledo: former capital of Castile

Excursion 3. Toledo

The city of Toledo is so rich in its history and culture that in a day you can sample only its principal sights; a morning walk around medieval streets and the judería takes about 3 hours; an afternoon visit to the cathedral 1 to 2 hours, depending on your interest.

– By car (N401), it takes only 40 minutes to Toledo. Trains leave every 2–3 hours (1 hour journey from Atocha or Chamartín); buses leave every 30 minutes from 6.30am, from the Estación Sur de Autobuses and take 1 hour. It is then 10 minutes by bus from either station into town –

A car is of no use once you're inside **Toledo**. To avoid crowds, go midweek and, preferably, arrive at the end of the day so you can get the feel of the town at night and early morning, before the first tourist buses arrive at 9.15am.

Spectacularly sited on a granite rock encircled by the river, Toledo is a microcosm of Spanish history: Roman fortress, Visigothic capital and centre of Muslim culture and learning, it reached the zenith of its power after it was reconquered by Alfonso VI in the 11th century and became capital of Castile. For over 3 centuries the Muslims, Jews and Christians lived side by side within its walls, producing a rich, hybrid culture. The court's transfer to Madrid in 1561 began the slow decline which also conserved its astonishing historical wealth.

Once inside the city walls, you're in a rabbit-warren of narrow streets, so it's a good idea to buy a city map from a newspaper stand. From the **Plaza de Zocodover**, where the buses from the train and bus stations arrive, go to the **Cristo de la Luz mosque**, the main monument from the early Arab period (kept locked, but you can get

Marzipan, Toledo's speciality

58

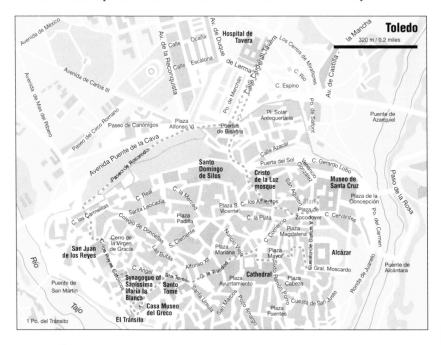

the key from Sr Manzano, the porter, who also acts as a guide for a small tip). Stepping over the fence, through the quiet garden, you arrive at the heights of the Puerta del Sol, with fine views to the north, looking down on two city gates, the Puertas de Bisagra Vieja and Nueva, Muslim and Renaissance respectively.

Close by (opposite the Puertas de Bisagra) is the **Hospital de Tavera** (10.30am–1.30pm and 3.30–6pm), worth visiting if you like palaces and painting – there are works by Titian, Ribera, Zurbarán, Tintoretto and El Greco, as well as a pharmacy, church, library and bedrooms with their 16th-century decoration. Make sure you ask to see the complete palace.

Returning to the Puertas de Bisagra, take the Paseo de Recaredo to the 11th-century Puerta de Cambrón, built by Alfonso VI, in which you can see the Arab inspiration under its present Renaissance style. Opposite is the Restaurante del Cardenal inside a 12th-century cardinal's palace, worth peeking into for an *aperitivo*. Close by, No 10 of the Puerta de Cambrón, is a shop selling regional products and offering tastings of Manchego cheese and local wine (prices are reasonable).

From here, the Cuesta de San Martín brings you out at **San Juan de los Reyes** (9am–noon, 3.30–6pm), one of a series of monasteries founded by Ferdinand and Isabel to commemorate their military

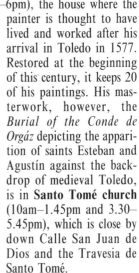

victories. The last major Gothic work in Toledo, it has kept its church, cloister and Arab entrance hall. Following Calle Reyes Católicos, you enter the *judería*, the old Jewish area of town, where a route is marked by red placards. In the strings of tourist souvenir shops, you may see the famous Toledan damascene steelwork being worked.

The prosperity and immunity of the Jewish community came to an abrupt end with the pogroms of 1355. In 1391 there was a massacre at the **Synagogue of Santísima María la Blanca** (10am–2pm and 3.30–6pm), the city's main synagogue in late medieval times. It was converted into a Christian church in the 14th century, but has been restored to its original state; the name comes from the white mortar of its walls. At the end of the street, on Paseo del Tránsito, is the second main synagogue, **El Tránsito** (10am–2pm and 4–6pm), founded by Samuel Levi, treasurer to Peter I, in 1366. The finest example of Toledan *mudéjar* architecture, its interior walls are covered by exquisite plasterwork from the Almohad period.

Close by, at Calle Samuel Levi 3, is the **Casa Museo del Greco** (Tuesday to Sunday 10am–2pm and 4–6pm), the house where the painter is thought to have lived and worked after his arrival in Toledo in 1577. Restored at the beginning of this century, it keeps 20 of his paintings. His masterwork, however, the *Burial of the Conde de Orgáz* depicting the apparition of saints Esteban and Agustín against the backdrop of medieval Toledo, is in **Santo Tomé church** (10am–1.45pm and 3.30–5.45pm), which is close by down Calle San Juan de Dios and the Travesia de Santo Tomé.

A good place to eat nearby is the **Asador Adolfo**, Calle Granada 6 (Tel: 227321; 1–4.30pm and 8pm–midnight), a restaurant in a 14th-cen-

Toledo by night

tury house where you can find new and traditional Toledan dishes, such as braised partridge and *carcamusa*, or braised pork.

In the afternoon, you can turn your attention to the **Cathedral** (3.30–6pm), one of the greatest monuments in Spain, with literally thousands of superb artistic and architectural details. To look round it properly takes at least 2 hours – and if you want to understand it fully, it is worth enlisting the services of a guide. The entrance ticket gives you access to the main body of the cathedral. Look out for the splendid carved walnut choir stalls; the frescoed Sala Capitular; the Sacristía Mayor, where there are various works by El Greco; and the Tesoro, a kind of church museum which spells out the church's extraordinary wealth and power. Also worth looking out for are the 16th-century stained-glass windows in the rose and side windows of the transept; the magnificent iron screens of the Capilla Mayor; and the opening in La Girola to let through natural light, known as the *Transparente*.

After so much visual richness, you're unlikely to have the energy for anything except a coffee and a piece of local marzipan. Nonetheless, much remains. If you stay overnight (*see Accommodation* under *Practical Information on p. 85*), another famous sight is the **Alcázar**, the fortress destroyed and rebuilt again and again from Roman times to the Civil War, when it was the setting for a famous scene of heroism. Architecturally, Charles V's fortress – reminiscent of El Escorial in style – dominates today, but it is very heavily restored, with reproduction armour. Close by is the **Museo de Santa Cruz**, a splendid Renaissance building which has great art exhibitions; and the **Convento de Santo Domingo de Silos**, the burial place of El Greco and his wife, where the nuns sell their own embroidery and handmade jewellery.

> ## Mudéjar Architecture
>
> *Mudéjar*, meaning literally 'surrendered or tributary', is the name given to the architectural style created by Muslim craftsmen who stayed in Spain after the Christian conquest. Muslim building and decorative techniques – Caliphal, Almohad and Nazari – were fused with Romanesque, Gothic and Renaissance features to produce Spain's most original architecture. The earliest *mudéjar* is found in Castile, most notably in Toledo, where the style reached a high-point from the 12th to the 16th centuries. The style was also adopted by the Jewish community after Christian persecution began in the 14th century.
>
> One characteristic of *mudéjar* architecture is the cheapness of its materials – brick, plaster, wood, roofing and ceramic tiles – used to highly decorative effect. Among its most notable features are tiers of pointed or horseshoe arches on minaret-type towers and belfries, and magnificent carved and painted wooden ceilings (*artesanados*).

If you do stay overnight you might want to explore the country to the south. A circular route can take you on the N401 via **Sonseca** (marzipan shops), **Orgáz** (14th-century palace-castle) and **Los Yebenes** (traditional leatherwork at Lolo, Plaza del Caudillo 10), past the Toledo mountains – source of the game you find in restaurants – and along the C402 and C403 to **La Puebla de Montalbán**, a historic small town.

Shopping

Shopping in Madrid is especially good for new-wave Spanish design, crafts, new and second-hand books and leather. The main shopping zones are: **Salamanca**, expensive and exclusive; **Gran Vía**, **Puerta del Sol** and **Princesa**, mid-price, with large department stores and Eurochains; the **old town**, particularly good for crafts.

Flamenco costumes in Calle San Jerónimo

Opening hours are flexible: 9am–2pm and 5–8pm or 8.30pm; department stores 10am–8pm, though many of the shops in the listing below open an hour later in the morning and close an hour later at night. Most also close on Saturday afternoons, with the exception of the big department stores, which open on Sundays before public holidays (useful but hell on earth).

Stores and Malls

El Corte Inglés, with branches at Calle Princesa 56, Calle Goya 76, Calle Preciados 3, Calle Raimundo Fernandez Villaverde 79 (tax refunds and shipping facilities, money change, travel agency, RENFE tickets and free maps) is Europe's most profitable – and one of its best – department stores.

There are three useful shopping malls for gift-buying: **Puerta de Toledo** (Ronda de Toledo 1; Tuesday to Saturday 11.30am–9pm, Sunday 11.30am–3pm); **Galería del Prado** (Plaza de las Cortes 7) with 40 luxury shops; **La Vaguada** (Metro Barrio del Pilar), a vast centre with 350 shops, restaurants and a food market. Branches of VIPS, a chain of drugstores, are open 9am–3am; central addresses are: Calle Fuencarral 158, Gran Vía 43, Calle Princesa 5, and, Calle Velázquez 84 and 136.

Bric-á-brac on the Calle Ribera de Curtidores

Antiques

Madrid's speciality is religious sculptures and objects; much else is imported and overpriced. Shops are grouped around Calle del Prado, and the Rastro, especially on Calle Ribera de Curtidores, which has antiques centres at Nos 12, 15 and 29. **Antigüedades** (Calle Segovia 16) is excellent. In November there is an antique fair, **Feriarte**, with a growing reputation.

Children

Fiestas Paco (Calle de Toledo 52) is a child's dream, with an extraordinary range of party disguises, masks, etc; opposite, at No 55, is **Caramelos Paco**, a huge sweet shop.

Books, Comics, Posters

Madrid is a mecca for book-lovers. The largest is **Espasa Calpe** (Gran Vía 29), but **Crisol** (Puerta de la Castellana 154, Goya 18 and Serrano 24; open till 10pm) is more pleasant for browsing. Specialist shops include **Fuentetaja** (San Bernardo 48) for literature and children's books, and **Estanislao Rodriguez** (No 27) for maps, bullfighting books and old prints. For second-hand books, try the stalls on **Cuesta de Moyano** (also open Sunday), or **Calle Libreros**; for old postcards, posters, etc, head for **Casa Postal** (Calle Libertad 37, 28004 Madrid; Tel: 5327037); for comics try **Totem** (Calle Gaztambide 20).

There is an antique book-fair in May, and a new book fair in El Retiro (24 May to 11 June).

Madrid is excellent for books

Crafts

Goatskin wine-bottles: **Julio Rodriguez** (Calle Aguila 12), founded 1907, now run by the third generation. Woodwork: **Florencio Cuadrado** (Ribera de Curtidores 35). Ceramics: tiles and other ceramics from all over Spain, **Antigua Casa de Talavera** (Calle Isabel la Catolica 2), founded in the 1920s, and boasting a wonderful tile facade. Kitchenware: **Alambique** (Plaza de Encarnación 2). Buttons, tassels, and trimmings: **El Botón de Oro** (Juan de Austria 33). Carpets, rugs and mats: original designs in cotton, jute and linen: **Alhaba Telar** (Buenavista 33). Haber-

Antigua Casa de Talavera

dashery: wonderful braids, lace, wools and trimmings from the shops in Plaza de Pontejos and Calle Espartero. Baskets, mats and brooms: **Espartería de Juan Sanchez** (Cuchilleros 9). Hats, uniforms, toy soldiers: **Casa Yustas** (Plaza Mayor 30). Guitar-maker: **Andrés Martín** (Calle Divino Pastor 22). Cork: **Corchera Castellana** (Calle Colegiata 4).

At **Artespana** (Don Ramón de la Cruz 33; Hermosilla 14) craft meets luxury design – beautiful but expensive. The **Puerta de Toledo** (see above) also has pricier designer crafts.

Records

Madrid Rock (Gran Vía 25) has a good flamenco section; **Real Musical** (Calle Carlos III 1) has classical and flamenco.

The ultimate in espadrilles at Alpargatería

Clothes and Fashion

Spanish dress and accessories can be found in small shops around the Puerta del Sol: **Casa de Diego** (Calle Montera 1) for fans; **Casa Jiménez** (Calle Preciados 52) for lace shawls, blankets; **Maty** (Calle Hileras 7) for flamenco clothes and dance shoes, and **Menkes** (Calle Mesonero Romanos 14) for flamenco and theatrical fabrics; **Sesena** (Calle de la Cruz 23), founded 1901, for capes (starting at a steep 62,000pesetas, but they last for a lifetime) as well as for fine embroidered shawls.

Spanish design names are on Calle Serrano (**Adolfo Dominguez**, No 96; **Loewe**, Nos 26 and 34) or close by – **Sybilla** is at Jorge Juan 12 (alley). Calle Almirante has good changing shops and **Zocco** (Galería del Prado, Plaza de las Cortes 7) specialises in young designers' work.

Shoes

For the best value, good quality shoes, go to **Calle Augusto Figueroa**, where shops sell direct from the factory; for high fashion, **Calle Almirante**; for *alpargatas* – espadrilles – of every conceivable kind, **Casa Vega** (Calle de Toledo 57) and the **Alpargatería** (Calle Divino Pastor 29); for high street prices and designs, **Calle Preciados** off Puerta del Sol.

Sweet sensation

Food and Drink

A good food souvenir is *turrón* – a honey sweetmeat which is first-cousin to Middle-Eastern *halva* but stickier and richer; the very best, bought by weight, comes from **Casa Mira** (Calle de San Jerónimo 30). Other edible items you might want to take home (for example saffron, regional liqueurs and wines, sausages, cheeses, preserves, olive oils) can be found in supermarkets or El Club de Gourmet departments of **El Corte Inglés** – pricey, but the one place to find everything under one roof.

Markets

The many municipal markets are open Monday to Saturday 8am–2pm and 5–8pm. In addition, there is the famous **Rastro street-market** on Sunday mornings (*see Option 6*). In some less central quarters, there are open-air markets on Saturday mornings for clothes, vegetables, lighting and pottery. In Plaza Mayor there is a Sunday morning **stamp-market**.

Madrid is a synthesis of the Spanish regions and this is reflected in its restaurants. The city is renowned for receiving the country's best produce by lorry through the night – or even, in the case of fish and seafood, by plane – so all the ingredients are on hand for the full gamut of regional cuisine, including Madrid's own *cocido* (*pot au feu* stew) in traditional taverns or *tascas*, Galician seafood and Mediterranean rices, traditional Basque and Asturian cooking, or, for those who like it, *nueva cocina* (nouvelle cuisine). International cuisine is, by contrast, badly represented and invariably disappointing.

A menu is usually broken down into *primeros platos* or *entrantes* (first courses); these might include *sopas* (soups), *mariscos* (shellfish), *revueltos* (scrambled eggs), *jamón* (chewy air-dried ham), *menestra* (braised vegetables), *pimientos* (peppers) and *queso* (cheese).

Segundos platos, or main courses, usually include *pescados* (fish), *carnes* (meat) and *caza* (game). They usually come without vegetables; if you want some, you need to ask for *verduras* (greens) or an *ensalada* (salad). Look out for *cordero* (lamb) and *perdíz* (partridge) among meats; among fish for *merluza* (hake), *rape* (monkfish), *besugo* (bream) and *bacalao* (saltcod) all common on menus. A *plato combinado* in cafeterias is simply a one-plate meal, complete with chips.

Postres, or desserts, will usually include the ubiquitous *flan* (créme caramel), *helados* (ice-

Flown in from the coast

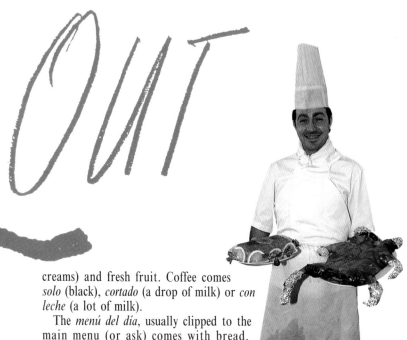

Chef at El Corcho

creams) and fresh fruit. Coffee comes
solo (black), *cortado* (a drop of milk) or *con leche* (a lot of milk).

The *menú del día*, usually clipped to the main menu (or ask) comes with bread, dessert and wine or water in the price.

Rioja, Navarra, Valdepeñas, Penedés and Ribera del Duero are the main wine denominations found in restaurants, although smaller ones (eg, Albariño, Rueda and Txacoli for white; Priorato and Ribeiro for red) are interesting to try.

If service and 12 percent IVA (VAT) are not included, this should be clearly stated on the menu.

The concentration of restaurants in the old town – around Plaza Santa Ana, in Centro behind Cibeles, and in the taverns of Cava Baja – includes establishments at every price level, from the 1,000pesetas lunchtime *menú del día* upwards (Zalacain, the city's top-rated restaurant, now clocks in at around £80 per head). *Tapas* mount up surprisingly too. Fish and seafood are of outstanding quality, but not cheap. Price categories below are based on a meal for one person with a bottle of wine: *$*= less than 4,000ptas; *$$*= 4,000–7,700ptas; *$$$*= more than 7,700ptas.

Unless you like an empty dining-room, you will need to adjust your stomach clock. Opening hours are usually around 1–4pm and 9–midnight, but *Madrileños* rarely lunch before 2 or 3pm, or book a dinner table for before 10pm (they fill the gaps with *tapas*). You'll often find a business lunch or dinner in progress at a neighbouring table – and not only in smart places if the kitchen turns out good food – but dress is casual. Tipping of 10 percent is usual.

Two final warnings: city-centre restaurants close on Sunday and for the month of August; exceptions are listed below. And a surprising number of restaurants don't take any credit cards; where this is the case, this is also mentioned below.

Nineteenth-century ambience at Lhardy's (see page 71)

Madrileñan Cooking

CASA SALVADOR
Calle Barbieri 12 (Metro Chueca)
Tel: 5214524
Since the 1950s a haunt of bankers and politicians at lunchtime, and artists and night-owls in the evening. Great squid, chicken *pepitoria* (braised chicken in an almond sauce), fish soups, hake, and wild boar – among a large choice. *$*

LA BOLA
Calle La Bola 5 (Metro Domingo/Opera)
Tel: 5476930
Famous for its *cocido*, cooked in tall earthenware pots over a wood fire (1,550ptas), and traditional family atmosphere. Book 1–2 days ahead. No credit cards; open on Sunday and no summer closing. *$*

LA PLAYA
Calle Magallanes 24 (Metro Quevedo)
Tel: 4468476
An unpretentious classic for home-cooking, with daily specials: *chard* (spinach blet) with potatoes, meat-balls, stuffed peppers, homemade puddings. No credit cards. *$*

POSADA DE LA VILLA
Calle Cava Baja 9 (Metro Tirso de Molina, Latina)
Tel: 2661860
One of the most attractive in a street of old inns, serving wood-roast lamb, tripe and other local dishes. Open for Sunday lunch. *$$*

TIENDA DE VINOS
Calle Augusto Figueroa 35 (Metro Chueca)
Tel: 5217012
A legendary eating house famed for its politics, generally known as La Comunista. Go for the atmosphere as much as the food. *$*

Other Regional Cooking

BALEAR
Calle Sagunto 18 (Metro Iglesia)
Tel: 4479115
Mediterranean *tapas* and meals with a Mallorcan bias. A good place to dip into the extensive range of rice-based options. *$*

EL CALDERO
Calle Huertas 15 (Metro Sol, Antón Martín), Tel: 4295044/0057

Refreshment at the ready

Sparkly clean family restaurant, serving Murcian cooking: fish baked in salt and *caldero* (rice and fish) are two specialities. Open for Sunday lunch. *$*

CASA GALLEGA
Calle Bordadores 11 and Plaza San Miguel 8 (Metro Sol/Opera)
Tel: 5419055 and 2473055
Of the many good Galician restaurants in Madrid, this one keeps down the prices of fish and shellfish without allowing the quality to drop. Octopus is a speciality here. Open Sundays and summer. *$*

CENTRO RIOJANO
Calle Serrano 25, 1st floor (Metro Goya/Serrano)
Tel: 5764852/5750337
A graceful dining-room, and excellent regional menu with *haute cuisine* touches (eg, pullet in wine vinegar, roasted peppers) and wide choice of Rioja wines. Very good value. Open Sunday lunch. *$*

EL CORCHO
Calle Zurbano 4
Tel: 3080136
Elegant but relaxed family restaurant, with light modern versions of

traditional dishes from around the country, and live music late Friday and Saturday. *$*

DE LA RIVA
Calle Cochabamba 13 (Metro Colombia/Principe de Vergara)
Tel: 2507757
Only open weekday lunchtimes, and always packed, but well worth the trip. Superb Castilian home-cooking – beans with partridge, *morcilla* (black sausage) with red peppers, braised vegetables and other dishes – plus house Ribera del Duero. *$*

EXTREMADURA
Calle Libertad 13 (Metro Chueca, Banco de España)
Tel: 5318958
Great lamb casseroles, wild vegetables, and a trayful of homemade *aguardientes* (eaux-de-vie) from Extremadura. Open Sunday lunch. *$*

EL LUARQUES
Calle Ventura de la Vega 16 (Metro Sol, Sevilla)
Tel: 4296174
One of the best of many Asturian restaurants: *fabada* (beans with meat and sausages) or *fabes con almejas* (beans with clams), hake cooked in cider, etc. Book ahead. *$$*

ZARAUZ
Calle Fuentes 13 (Metro Opera)
Tel: 5477270

Snails a speciality

Traditional tapas bar

Traditional Basque cooking: roast sea-bream or salt-cod dishes (such as *al pil-pil* or *a la vizcaina*), plus *txakolí*, a Basque white wine. Open Sunday lunch. *$$*

Gourmet Cuisine

CABO MAYOR
Calle Juan Ramón Jimenez 37 (Metro Cuzco)
Tel: 2508776
Superb *nueva cocina* fish and vegetables, cooked Cantabrian style, and a relaxed but chic atmosphere. Summer terrace. *$$*

ZALACAIN
Calle Alvarez Baena 4 (Metro Rubén Darío)
Tel: 5615935
The first ever Spanish restaurant to get three Michelin stars and still rated by many as the best in the country, with inspired Basque-Navarrese *haute cuisine*, a superb cellar, excellent formal service – and, inevitably, prices to match. *$$$*

Other Cuisines

AL-MOUNIA
Puerta Recoletos 6 (Metro Retiro/ Banco de España)
Tel: 4350828
Moroccan cooking turned into a one-off experience by a wonderful tiled interior. *$$*

ZARA
Calle Infantas 5 (Metro Gran Vía)
Tel: 5322074
Cuban food, and great cocktails; very relaxed. Book ahead. *$*

Vegetarian

Vegetarian dishes are thin on the ground, although *tortilla de patatas* is nearly always available. The few vegetarian restaurants (all inexpensive) include: **El Vegetariano** (Maqués de Santa Ana 34, Tel: 5320927; Metro Noviciado/Tribunal), with a changing seasonal menu and salad bar; **Artemisa** (Calle Ventura La Vega 4, Tel: 4295092), always busy; **La Granja** (Calle San Andrés 11, Tel: 5328798; Metro Bilbao/Tribunal), macrobiotic.

Tapas Routes

Spanish food is best known abroad for its *tapas* (bar snacks akin to Greek *mezze*). They come in three sizes: *pinchos* (one mouthful), *tapas* (small snack) and *raciones* (platefuls). Since the whole point of *tapas* is to *tapear* (hop from one place to the next) I have arranged the following recommendations according to area. They span the spectrum of *tapas* bars, from elegant to earthy. The best times to go to catch everywhere open is noon–2pm, and 8–10.30pm.

PLAZA SANTA ANA
A classic *tapas* route, given to me by a Madrid veteran, is as follows: **La Toscana** (corner Ventura de la Vega/

Manuel Fernández y González), *morcilla de ternera* (veal sausage); **La Chuleta** (Calle Echegaray 20), griddled mushrooms or baby lamb chops; **La Venencia** (Calle Echegaray 7), marinated olives, salt-dried tuna); **Garrabatu** (Calle Echegaray 5), Asturian cider, stuffed potatoes or onions; **La Trucha** (Manuel Fernández y González 3), fried fish, perhaps in *adobo* (marinated), or brains; **Bar Vina P** (Plaza Santíssima Ana 3), squid or mussels; **La Casa del Abuelo** (Nuñez de Arce 5), prawns *a la plancha* and sweetbreads; **El Otro Abuelo** (Calle Victoria 12) *jamón serrano* – cured ham.

PUERTA DEL SOL

Casa Bravas (Pje de Matheu 5), where Madrid's most famous *tapa*, *patatas bravas* (roasted potatoes with peppery sauce), was invented and the recipe for the peppery sauce is still kept a secret; **Lhardy's** (San Jerónimo 8), 19th-century elegance, real consommé from samovars and croquettes from glass cabinets; **Casa Labra** (Calle Tetuán 12), where Pablo Iglesias founded the Socialist Party, famous for its salt-cod.

CENTRO

El Bocaíto (Libertad 6), which some Madrileños rate as the best in Madrid, inventive, upmarket and pricey; **Bar Santander** (Calle Augusto Figueroa 25), with *migas* (fried breadcrumbs) as well as canapés and quiches; **Cerveceria Sta Bárbara** (Plaza Santa Bárbara 8, Tel: 3190499), shellfish and beer; **El Timón** (Calle de Orellana 19), shellfish.

BILBAO

Calles Cardenal Cisneros and **Hartzenbusch**, more studenty and cheaper than the other areas and offering everything from Andalucian fried fish – at **La Giralda** (Hartzenbusch 12 and 15) – to pigs' ears, a Madrid favourite.

La Trucha in Santa Ana

Nightlife

Madrid is one of the best places in Europe for a night on the razzle. I should warn you that prices are high – 800pesetas upwards in anywhere with music and classy design – and that taxis are hard to pick up on the street by 4am; so call a radiotaxi before leaving a venue.

When in the 1980s Madrid's nightlife was deemed the most exciting in Europe, it was not as newsworthy as outsiders seemed to think. Even the 1202 *fuero*, the first body of local laws, had tried to limit excessive late-night noise, and by the 17th century, the halcyon age of court revelry, every third day was reputed to be a fiesta. In the 19th century, Pérez Galdós, describing Calle Montera off the Puerta del Sol, captured the atmosphere of this: 'the animation was, as always, excessive. It is the mouth of a river of people which chokes against a rising human tide.'

Reveller in Manolo's, Malasaña

Today the 1980s urge to make up for lost time after the repression of Franco's years has lost much of its fizz. But Madrid's nightlife remains a phenomenon to be seen at least once, if only to witness the famous 4am traffic jams and to see the *Madrileños* in their element. You will very rarely encounter any aggression.

The key idea to a Madrileñan night is to hop around, depending on the time and what you're looking for. A friend from Madrid

72

The city is electric by night

once joked that you cannot say you have been out for *tapas* unless you have done at least half the number of the stations of the cross – that is, seven bars. It is this restlessness, half spontaneous and half ritualistic, which forms the basis of Madrid's long nights.

The addresses that follow are offered as a core from which to start, but bear in mind that Madrid has over 30,000 bars, and that if you are doing things in the Madrileñan spirit there is no such thing as a fixed plan. Early evening – that is, 8 or 9pm – is the ideal time to *tapear*, before places are too full, or to visit some of the traditional taverns and *bodegas*. It isn't until after dinner or the cinema, around 11.30pm–midnight, that people begin to move off to the more fashionable music bars (it's hard to get wine in these) and not until 1–2am that they make it to the dance floors.

Around this time of night, when an army of street-cleaners hose down the streets, you remember the old motto '*Madrid me mata*' (Madrid kills me). Bad driving habits, the *Madrileños'* boisterous stamina, and conspicuous consumption can all get you down. Drinks, too, get stronger as the night goes on. If you're flagging, a *carajillo* (coffee with a slug of cognac) comes in handy.

In summer, a more relaxing option is a *terraza*, one of the big open-air terrace-bars. These were the hub of nightlife in the late 1980s, turning over up to 5 million pesetas a day from the sale of drinks – everything from *horchata* (tiger nut milk) and coffee to *cubatas* (gin or whisky and coke), a favourite *madrileño* tipple.

If you make it through to the early hours, then you can end the night the traditional way with thick, sweet, drinking chocolate and *churros* at **Chocolatería San Ginés**, Pasadizo de San Ginés 5, open midnight–7am. And if you stick the pace right through to the morning, have an *anis* or cognac to *matar el gusanillo* – kill the worm – as the saying goes, at one of the 24-hour kiosks such as El Arbol, on the corner of Moncloa with the Parque del Oeste.

Traditional Taverns

Madrid has kept a large number of its traditional bars, which are some of the best places to soak up the city's character. This is a brief selection, grouped according to area:

IN THE CENTRO:
Angel Sierra (Plaza de Chueca 1), wonderful old tiled bar serving vermouth and beer on tap (the square can feel threatening after

dark); **Bodegas la Ardosa** (Calle Colón 13 and Calle Santa Engracia 70), a range of beers and vermouth on tap from barrels, characterful decor; **Manolo** (Calle Jovellanos s/n, opposite theatre), classic 1930s bar.

IN SALAMANCA:
Pelaez (Calle Lagasca 61), one of the few typical bars left in the area. Great canapés and waiters with *hauteur*.

IN THE PLAZA DE ESPAÑA:
El 51 (Calle Princesa 51), with tiles showing the seven wonders of the world, beer on tap and good *empanadas*.

IN THE OLD TOWN:
Taberna de Antonio Sanchez (Calle Mesón de Paredes 13), classic bullfighting and artists' bar with *tapas* and restaurant; **Cayetano** (Calle Encarnacion 13, near the Rastro), great prawns; **Cuevas de Luis Candelas** (Escalerilla de Piedra s\n, opposite theatre), now very touristy with regional songs, etc, on tap; **El 21**

Taberna de Antonio Sanchez

(Calle Toledo 21), picturesquely messy, with beer crates on the bar, liqueurs from all over the world and great deep-fried squid.

Bars

Madrid nightlife and culture is more about bars and alcohol than anything else. Below are a few of the perennials in the main areas – **Centro, Malasaña, Plaza Santa Ana, Moncloa** (students). The peak time to go is marked in brackets where relevant. Prices are killing: expect to pay from 800–1,000ptas a drink in anywhere with music and decor. The *Guía del Ocio*, sold in all kiosks, is the only listings magazine.

Close to the street: **Agapo** (Calle Madera 22), indispensable rock 'n' roll dive; **La Iguana** (Calle Hernán Cortés 12), more sophisticated but with less history; **La Vía Lactea** (Calle Velarde 18), a reliable '70s classic that never goes out fashion, with snooker, flipper

and table football; **Templo de Gato** (Calle Trujillos 7), more claus-
trophobic but with some live music; **Fábrica de Pan** (Calle San
Bartolome 21), with a real fire in winter.

For Madrid's bronzed yuppies: **Hanoi** (Calle Hortaleza 81), the
most moneyed; **Bagatelle** (Calle Barquillo 44), in better taste, with
varied public and music; **Teatriz** (Calle Hermosilla 15), with flash
Philippe Starck decor; **El Cock** (Calle de la Reina 16), eclectic
yuppy and art crowd.

Ex-*Movida* haunts: **Ambigú** (Calle Leganitos 25), full of corridors
and niches (2–3am); **Torero Torero**, Calle La Cruz 26 (open till
6am), more young-bourgeois and image-conscious (the doorman
doesn't let many people in).

Quiet havens: **Libertad 8**, at that address, with piped classical
music or live piano when people feel moved to play; **Palacio de
Gaviria** (Calle Arenal 9), more expensive but the historic 19th-cen-
tury backdrop is fantastic.

Terrazas

The summer terraces, sometimes with live music or
street theatre, are a
unique characteristic of
Madrid's nightlife, but
fading fast without the
support of the city council.
The action moves on every
summer, so you need to ask.
There are some perennials in great
settings: **El Aguilar** (Calle de Bustamante),
with a dozen bars in a street of old warehouses;
the patio of the **Cuartel Conde Duque** (Calle del Conde Duque).
Those along the Castellana are slick, elegant and pricey; those on
Rosales, by the park, cool, breezy and more traditional. **El Arbol**,
on the junction of Puerta de Moret and Princesa, is open 24 hours
a day in summer, and all year.

Club-goers in Malasaña

Dancing

Big names are **Joy Eslava** (Calle Arenal 12), with plush blue-velvet
theatrical decor and lots of corporate parties, and **Pachá** (Calle
Barceló 11), now well off-the-boil. There's fun to be had at **Villa
Rosa** (on the corner of Nuñez del Arco/Calle Alvarez Gato);
Keeper (Calle Juan Bravo 48), popular with out-of-town yuppies;
Die Mahuer (Calle Arturo Soria 195), spacious with mainstream
music; **El Sol** (Calle Jardines 3), popular with the film world; **Stella**
(Calle Alarban 7), a roller-disco owned by singer Alaska, which
draws a big gay crowd and a few locally famous faces (2–7am); **Bo-
caccio** (Calle Marques de la Ensenada 16), plenty of plush red vel-
vet, various atmospheres in a *belle epoque* setting and a full dance-
floor; **El 42** (Calle Claudio Coello 42), 1960s soundtrack; **Morocco**

(Calle Marques de Leganés 7), also owned by Alaska.

Madrid is strong on salsa. A few addresses are: **Habana** (Calle San Vicente Ferrer 23), where 40-year-olds try to keep in rhythm; **Calentito** (Calle Jacometrezo 15), small and fun though the dancers on the bar bring voyeurs, and **Oba-Oba**, opposite, with tacky decor but real Brazilians; **Café del Mercado** (Mercado Puerta de Toledo), where you find divorced, single and adulterous 30–40-somethings looking for action.

There are also some amusing dance-halls. At **La Carroza** (Calle Flor Baja 8), 60-year-olds look for romance; **Dos Gardenias** (Avenida General Perón 34; 7–10.30pm) has an orchestra.

Arts Festivals

Many cultural events take place within the umbrella of arts and theatre festivals, such as **Imagfic**, science-fiction cinema (April); classical ballet (December to January); flamenco (April); international theatre (March to April). The **Autumn Festival** combines concerts, theatre, opera and ballet (September to October). For most events, tickets are available only from the venue itself 5 days ahead. **Localidades Galicia** (Plaza del Carmen 1, Tel: 5312732) is a theatrical ticket agency; **Discoplay** (Calle Princesa 1 and Calle Hernani 57) does tickets for rock concerts.

Music

For classical music, the **Auditorio Nacional de Musica** (Calle Principe de Vergara 146, Tel: 3370100) has excellent programming. For opera, *zarzuela* – a Spanish form of operetta, dance and other musical events, the main venues until the opening of the Teatro Real in 1995 are the **Teatro de la Zarzuela** (Jovellanos 4, Tel: 4298225), and **Centro Cultural de la Villa** (Plaza de Colón, Tel: 5756080).

There is no real native contemporary music scene. **Revolver** (Calle Galileo 26) brings over some interesting bands; **Yasta** (Calle Valverde 10) is a good small venue though the music varies in quality; **Café Central** (Plaza del Angel 10) is a jazz landmark, always packed, expensive and a bit pedantic. **La Coquette** (Calle Hileras 14) is the

Joy Esclava disco

most authentic blues dive, and **La Fídula** (Calle Huertas 57) has piped or live classical music.

Gay

The Madrid gay scene is frenetic. Because it's fashionable and the best dance scene, you find quite a few women in the clubs. Reliable places to start are **Black and White** (Calle Libertad 14), with live shows, and **Ales** (Calle de la Venera 6); then ask there where's new. Smaller bars are mainly in Centro: for example, **Trafic** (Calle Reina 2) and **Leather** (Calle Pelayo 42).

Cinema and Theatre

Subtitled movies (labelled, v.o.) are plentiful. Main venues are the **Alphaville** and **Renoir** (Calle Martín de los Heros 12 and 14), and **Idealmulticines** (Calle Dr Cortazo 6); they do early morning sessions on Fridays and Saturdays.

Theatre is usually in Spanish, except during the autumn festival of theatre.

Cabaret and Flamenco

Madrid has a strong flamenco tradition, but the *tablaos*, or shows, are commercial: **Café de Chinitas** (Calle Torija 7); **Corral de la Pacheca** (Calle Juan Ramón Jiménez 26); newer, and well done, is **Florida Park** (Avenida Melendez Pelayo/Retiro Park, Tel: 5737804; 9pm–3am). If you speak Spanish, **Noches del Cuplé** (Calle Palma 51, Tel: 4165683), with Olga Ramos, veteran singer, is a must. All cost at least 4,000ptas.

El Café del Foro (Calle San Andrés 38), decorated like a miniature village, has travelling cabaret and magicians, while at **King Kong** (Calle Trujillos 3), the owner directs, designs the sets and acts. The **Ruta del Terror** (Balcon de Rosales, 9pm–3am) is an amusing human ghost train.

There are literally dozens of sex shows (and some of the largest sex shops in Europe). Among these is a women-only male strip at **Charles** (Calle Principe de Vergara 66); and a comic porn show for men in **Erika** (Silva 10). Prostitutes are openly available in Calle La Cruz, Ballesta and Desengano, cheap; Calle Capitán Haya upmarket.

Gambling

The **Casino**, although one of the biggest in Europe – 14 roulette wheels – is antiseptic in atmosphere and a long way out – Carretera de la Coruña *kilómetro* 28,300. Free buses (N6) from Plaza España. You need official identification to get in.

Hipódromo

The summer races at the **Hipódromo de la Zarzuela** (Carretera de La Coruna *kilómetro* 7,800; Tel: 3070140) are an evening social event. Days vary each year; phone to check. Entry 300–1,000ptas.

Calendar of Special Events

Like every Spanish city, Madrid is enjoying a revival of its fiestas, which now include solemn religious processions, over 80 *verbenas* (neighbourhood street-parties) between June and September; and a cultural and sports calendar. Here are a few of the main attractions in Madrid; check what else is going on when you arrive.

JANUARY

Los Reyes Magos: On the night of 5 January, the Three Kings parade through town – arriving by helicopter, camel, etc.
San Antón: At the church in Calle Hortaleza, the blessing of animals takes place on 17 January, San Antón's feast day.

FEBRUARY

Carnaval: Banned for 50 years by Franco as a threat to public order, Carnival (from the end of February) has come back in an uninhibited way, with masked costume (in parades, at parties, on the street), drinking, much transsexual dressing, concerts, etc.

The most traditional part is the Ash Wednesday **Burial of the Sardine** (San Antonio de la Florida), a mock funeral and bonfire.

MARCH

ARCO: One of Europe's largest and most avant-garde contemporary art fairs, visited by thousands of Spaniards (early March).
Easter: Madrid's Semana Santa processions are in the solemn Castilian tradition where religious images are taken out of the churches and paraded through the streets. The most noteworthy processions are outside Madrid: Chinchón's medieval passion play on Good Friday; Cuenca's dawn Procession of the Borrachos (drunks); Toledo's, Avila's and Segovia's atmospheric silent processions against medieval backdrops.

MAY

Segundo Mayo: The commemoration of the 1808 rising against Napoleon is a big local holiday, marked by sports events, concerts, etc.

Columbus Day celebrations

San Isidro: Madrid's biggest fiestas are for its patron saint. From 8–15 May, the city is alive with *verbenas*, a bullfight season (the most important in the world), a jazz festival, marathon, open-air theatre, and huge *cocido* cooked in the Plaza Mayor.

In Lavapiés and various other quarters, the custom of **May Queens** has been revived.

On the 15th, the cyclists of the **Vuelta de España** – like the Tour de France – finish in the Paseo de la Castellana.

JUNE

San Antonio de la Florida: On 13 June, single women file into the church to offer a pin in the hope of finding a boyfriend; outside is a big street party.

AUGUST

San Cayetano (7 August), **San Lorenzo** (10), **La Paloma** (15): the most *castizo* of all the Madrileñan fiestas. In all of them, Virgins are taken out of the neighbourhood churches and paraded through the streets, and the *chotis* is danced to the *organillo* – sometimes in old Madrileñan costume.

DECEMBER

Christmas: During December, the Plaza Mayor has a market selling Nativity figures and decorations. Christmas Eve is spent at home, but New Year's Eve is one of the biggest nights out of the year, with thousands in the Puerta del Sol for the traditional eating of 12 grapes when the clock strikes midnight.

Easter penitents' procession

Atocha Station

GETTING THERE

By Air

Most international airlines have flights to Madrid. The airport (Barajas) is 16km (10 miles) from the city centre; buses leave for Plaza Colón every 15 minutes. A taxi will set you back about 2,000ptas. From 1994, a 20-minute rail-link will run from Barajas to mid-town Nuevos Ministerios.

By Rail

Two trains leave Paris every night: the Expreso Puerta del Sol, which has turn-of-the-century decor, couchettes, and carries cars; and the Talgo Camas/couchette, more modern and comfortable, with beds. Both arrive at **Chamartín station**, from where you can get the Metro or a taxi to the centre.

By Road

The car journey from London and northern Europe takes a minimum of 24 hours (in a fast car, without an overnight break). Allow 6 hours from the Spanish border at Irún to Madrid. Burgos is a good stop-off to visit the magnificent cathedral and eat well. You need a green card, log book and bail bond, and it's advisable to carry an International Driving Permit.

By Sea

There is a ferry from Britain to Spain (Plymouth to Santander, journey time 24 hours). The convenience has to be balanced against the cost, and in winter the risk of cancellations because of bad weather. The service stops for three weeks at Christmas. Information: Brittany Ferries, Milbay Docks, Plymouth PL1 3EF, Tel: 0752 221321. From Santander, you can drive to Madrid via Reinosa, Palencia and Valladolid, taking in fine Romanesque architecture.

TRAVEL ESSENTIALS

When to Visit

The main factor is the weather (see below). In August, the city is pleasantly empty, though small shops and restaurants tend to be closed. By the first week, the worst of the heat has broken.

Passports and Customs

Standard EC regulations apply: passports are not needed for visits of up to 3 months.

Weather

Madrid's climate is often summed up in the old adage, 'six months of *invierno* (winter) and three months of *infierno* (hell)'. This is an exaggeration: there are two to three weeks of hell (mid-July to the beginning of August), but outside that the dryness makes bearable average daily temperatures of over 30°C/86°F (and up to 45°C/110°F) in summer and just below zero in winter. Rainwear isn't vital – it rains about 50 days a year – but sunglasses are essential. When the air is still, pollution is heavy.

Clothing

Madrileños may be casually elegant, overtly sexy, or formally bejewelled, but they are always conformist dressers. Street fashion hardly exists and deliberate scruffiness is not understood or liked. Flesh exposure is okay, but beachwear is inappropriate.

Electricity

The voltage is 225AC though a few old buildings still have 125 volts. Two round-pin plugs are standard everywhere, so bring an adaptor if yours are 3-pin or the American flat pin.

Time Differences

Madrid is an hour ahead of Greenwich Mean Time. Noon in Madrid is 11am in London, 6am in New York, 3am in Los Angeles, and 9pm in Sidney. In winter darkness falls around 6pm; in mid-summer 10pm.

GETTING ACQUAINTED

Geography

Madrid is the highest capital in Europe (650m/2,130ft), sitting in a dish in the central Iberian plateau, flanked to the north and east by the sierras of Somosierra and Guadarrama, and to the southeast by those of Toledo. The compact city centre is spread over hillocks, with the diminutive River Manzanares running round them to the south. In the last 20 years, huge suburbs dissected by motorways running into the centre have grown around the city.

Government and Economy

Spain is a parliamentary monarchy, ruled by King Juan Carlos I de Borbón and governed since 1982 by the socialists (PSOE) with Felipe González as President. Madrid – the country's political, administrative and economic capital – is currently in the hands of the rival conservatives (PP). The city's economy, based on industrialisation since the 1950s, has been fuelled by heavy foreign investment, especially in advanced technologies.

Religion

The majority religion is Catholic, though fewer than 25 percent of Spaniards regularly go to church. Some Catholic churches give foreign language Masses; Madrid also has the largest mosque in Europe (M-30), a synagogue (Calle Balmes 3) and Anglican church (St George's, Calle Hermosilla 45) among 50 non-Catholic churches in the city.

San José church

Spoiling for a bullfight

who live in *chabolas* (shanty-towns); Moroccans, who provide cheap labour for building and, more recently, other Africans and South Americans.

Currency

The peseta comes in coins – some irritatingly small – of 1, 5, 25, 100, 200 and 500 pesetas, and notes from 1,000 up to 10,000ptas. People often talk in *duros*, which are worth 5ptas.

Credit cards

A surprising number of restaurants and shops don't take cards. Visa is the most widely accepted, then Access/Mastercard. You may also have difficulty paying with Eurocheques.

Telebanco cash machines (outside many banks) accept most of the usual cards, but often run out of notes at the end of the month, or at weekends. If you are going out of Madrid for the day, it's best to get cash before you leave. Help numbers: Amex 2796200; Diners 2474000; Mastercard 5192100; Visa 5192100.

Tipping

Although service is included in all bills, it is usual to tip in bars and restaurants,

How Not to Offend

Spaniards have an easy-going, familiar kind of courtesy based on common sense rather than etiquette, but they tend to be defensive when criticised or laughed at. If you are speaking Spanish, use the formal *usted*, rather than informal *tú*, for you.

Population

On top of the city's 3 million residents and the province's 5–6 million residents recorded in the census, there are many more without legal existence: the gypsies,

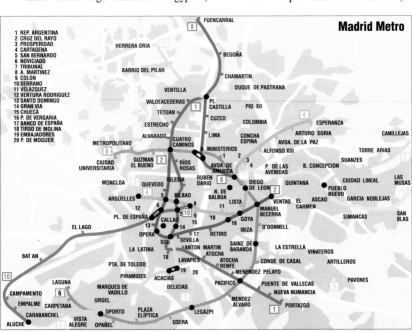

Madrid Metro

1 REP. ARGENTINA
2 CRUZ DEL RAYO
3 PROSPERIDAD
4 CARTAGENA
5 SAN BERNARDO
6 NOVICIADO
7 TRIBUNAL
8 A. MARTINEZ
9 COLON
10 SERRANO
11 VELAZQUEZ
12 VENTURA RODRIGUEZ
13 SANTO DOMINGO
14 GRAN VIA
15 CHUECA
16 P. DE VERGARIA
17 BANCO DE ESPAÑA
18 TIRSO DE MOLINA
19 EMBAJADORES
20 P. DE MOGUER

to guides, taxi-drivers, hotel and station porters, hairdressers and ushers. The size of the tip can vary; from 5–10 percent in a restaurant down to 2–3 percent in a taxi. It is more offensive to give too small a tip than none.

Changing Money

Banks are open Monday to Friday 9am–2pm, with a few city-centre branches open Saturday. Outside these hours, you can change money in Barajas airport, Chamartín and Atocha railway stations, and most four- and five-star hotels. Central Madrid – Gran Vía, Puerta del Sol etc – also has money-changers (only buying foreign currencies), among which **Check Point**, Plaza Callao 4, is open 24 hours a day.

GETTING AROUND

Street numbers always run outwards from the Puerta del Sol, with even numbers on the right and odd on the left.

Taxis

There are more than 15,000 taxis in Madrid. White with a red diagonal strip, they show a green light on the roof and hang a *Libre* sign in the front window when free. Some operate only as a telephone service (eg, **Radioteléfono**: 547 8200). The fare shown on the meter is subject to supplements shown on a notice in the back: eg, 300ptas to or from the airport; 50ptas for each suitcase; 150ptas between 11pm and 6am and on public holidays.

Metro

The quickest way of moving around the city, safe and clean, the Metro runs 6am–1.30am. The 10 lines (120 stations) are labelled by number, colour and final

Buses run from 6am–midnight

destination. Bulk buying tickets for 10 journeys saves up to 50 percent. You can get a Metro map at the ticket booth.

Train

Suburban trains operate 5.30am–11pm. There are nine lines to commuter towns etc, and the main inter-city lines, from three stations: **Chamartín** (for Barcelona, all international trains, Cadíz); **Atocha** (for Seville by AVE – the new high-speed train, Aranjuez, Toledo, Alcalá de Henares and Guadalajara); **Príncipe Pío/Norte** (for Avila, Galicia, Asturias). These stations are linked by Metro. Phone bookings, Tel: 5013333; Information, Tel: 5300202. The RENFE Central Office, Gran Vía 44, is open 9.30am–8pm.

Bicycles can be taken on suburban trains only.

Bus

There are more than 150 routes in red and yellow air-conditioned buses, which run from 6am–midnight. Tickets for both are a flat price. A reduced-price ticket for 10 journeys can be bought in an *estanco* (tobacconist's/newspaper kiosk). Radial night services leave on the hour from Cibeles and the Puerta del Sol. Buses for out-of-town trips, belonging to various private companies, go mainly from the **Estación Sur de Autobuses** (Calle Canarias 17, Tel: 4673577; Metro Palos de la Frontera), but check first.

Car

Driving in Madrid is not recommended: chronic traffic jams, anarchic parking, full car-parks, and frequent road-works kill your nerves. Never leave a radio or luggage in the car, even in an underground car-park. A car is a blessing for

out-of-town trips, provided you avoid the four daily rush hours (going in 7.30–9.30am, and at 5pm; going out 2–3pm and 8–9.30pm). Beware of on-the-spot speeding fines.

To hire a car, you need to be over 21 and have a current driving licence. Offices are at the airport or in the city centre (**Hertz**, Calle Jacometrezo 15, Tel: 5421000 and **Europcar**, Calle Orense 29, Tel: 5559930). A deposit is required unless you pay by credit card.

HOURS & HOLIDAYS

From September to June, most office hours are 8am–2pm and 5–7pm. In summer all offices and some shops extend the morning to 3pm and then close in the afternoons. From the end of July, when *Madrileños* go on holiday to escape the heat, many smaller businesses are closed.

National holidays are: 1 and 6 January, 19 March, Good Friday, 1 May, 15 August, 12 October, 1 November, 6 and 25 December. Local holidays are: 2 and 15 May, 6 November, 7 and 8 December. The city is very quiet during Easter Week, but less so at Christmas.

ACCOMMODATION

The selection below spans Madrid's wide price range, with an emphasis on character. All hotels are required to display prices (including service and tax) at reception and in each bedroom, and to keep a complaints book (*Hoja Oficial de Reclamaciones*). Staying out of town can be a good option; it is much cheaper for the standard of accommodation, and promises peace and quiet. For help in

A suite at the Ritz

finding hotels contact the tourist information desk at the airport or in the Plaza de España. Prices given below are for double rooms. $ = 6,000–12,000ptas; $$ = 12,000–19,000ptas; $$$ = above 19,000ptas.

Madrid

Hotels

AROSA
Calle de la Salud 21, Metro Gran Vía
Tel: 5321600
Friendly four-star hotel, just off the Gran Vía. Attracts tour groups. $$

DON DIEGO
Calle Velázquez 45, Metro Velázquez
Tel: 4350760
Good value three-star hotel in uptown Salamanca. $

FRANCISCO I
Calle Arenal 15, Metro Sol, Opera
Tel: 5480204
Old-fashioned hotel near old Madrid. $

INGLÉS
Calle Echegaray 10, Metro Sevilla
Tel: 4296551
Near Plaza Sta Ana, theatreland and old Madrid. Three-star hotel with garage. $

MONACO
Calle Barbieri 5, Metro Chueca, Gran Vía
Tel: 5224630
Once a classy whorehouse, now an excellent 2-star hotèl, this is a bargain for the standard and quirky decor of the rooms. Bar and breakfast café only, but you are right in restaurant land. $

RITZ
Plaza de la Lealtad, 5
Tel: 521 2857
Old-style luxury near the Prado. $$$

SANVY
Calle Goya 3, Metro Colón
Tel: 5760800
Just off Plaza Colón, quiet and comfortable four-star hotel used by Spanish businessmen, with a pool, fitness centre, and one of the best hotel restaurants. $$$

Serrano Husa
Calle Marqués de Villamejor 8, Metro Serrano
Tel: 4355200
Small and exclusive in an old-world way, in uptown Salamanca. A four-star hotel, but public rooms are small. *$$*

Tirol
Calle Marqués de Urquijo 4, Metro Arguelles
Tel: 5481900
Good value, three-star hotel famous for its cocktails and right next to Parque del Oeste. *$*

Wellington
Calle Velázquez 8, Metro Goya, Retiro
Tel: 5754400
If you want luxury, this is the most atmospheric (early 1950s) five-star hotel, tastefully subdued and with strong bullfighting connections. Right by the Retiro Park. *$$$*

Hostales
Hostales and *pensiónes* are found all round Madrid for around 1,500–4,000ptas a night, depending on whether or not you share a bathroom. A good place to start looking is Plaza Santa Ana, where you'll find several on every street.

Pedro Romero Cortes
Calle Fernando VI 5–8, Metro Alonso Martínez
Tel: 319 40 46
Clean and comfortable.

Youth Hostel
Recinto Casa de Campo
Metro Lago
Tel: 4635699
You need to be a member; maximum three-night stay. Reduced cost for people under 26.

Camping
Camping Osuna
Avenida de Logrono s/n, Metro Canillejas
Tel: 7410510
Set in shade-giving pine trees, it has a bar, restaurant, play-park, food shop, and bungalows; rates are low. Open all year round. No buses.

Out of Town

Chinchon
Parador de Turismo de Chinchon
Calle Generalísimo 1, Tel: 91 8940836
45km (28 miles) from Madrid. A converted 17th-century monastery with beautiful garden and pool; the small historic town, inundated at weekends, has a beautiful *plaza*, church and good restaurants. Packed at Easter for the medieval Passion play. *$$*

Rascafría
Santa Maria de El Paular
Rascafría, Tel: 91 8691011
94km (58 miles) from Madrid. Luxury four-star hotel within Spain's first Carthusian monastery, set against the sierra. Rooms overlooking the cloister. Contains one of Buñuel's favourite bars. *$$*

Segovia
El Hidalgo
Calle José Canalejas 3–5, Tel: 911 428190
Restored medieval palace with only seven rooms. Clean and cheap. Meals are served in a beautiful cloister. Hostal prices.

Los Linajes
Calle Doctor Velasco 9, Tel: 911 431712
Well converted inside an old palace. Good views and close to the Plaza Mayor. *$*

Sigüenza
Hostal el Doncel
Puerta de la Alameda, Tel: 911 390001
Simple, clean and within easy walking distance of both the old town and the station. Good restaurant. Hostal prices.

Parador de Turismo de Sigüenza
El Castillo, Tel: 911 390100
Within 17th-century bishop's palace-castle at the top of the town. Great furnishings and garden. *$*

Toledo
Hostal del Cardenal
Puerta de Recaredo 24, Tel: 925 224900
Historic three-star hotel, built by Cardenal Lorenzana in the 18th century. Excellent restaurant. *$*

General Health

The water in Madrid is good, although there is heavy inner-city pollution. Winter dryness often provokes cold sores and sinus troubles.

Pharmacies

A green or red cross identifies a chemist (*farmacia*). Spanish pharmacists are highly trained paramedics, and are able to deal with many minor ailments. You can freely buy many medicines, including antibiotics, that are available only on prescription in other countries. Outside shop hours go to a *farmacia de guardia*, listed in chemist's windows and in the newspaper. You can also find the nearest *farmacia de guardia* by dialling 098.

Medical/Dental Services

If you are an EC citizen and have an E111 form, you will be treated free at *Urgencias* – casualties – in one of the large hospitals or at one of the local Ambulatorios, which are open 24 hours a day (addresses in the windows of pharmacies and in the newspapers). Given long waiting lists and potential expenses, it is a good idea to have private medical insurance. Dental services are not covered by the Spanish national health, and are expensive. The **Anglo-American Medical Unit** (Calle Conde de Aranda 1, Tel: 4351823) gives bilingual attention 24 hours a day.

Crime/Lost Property

Street crime is pretty much as in any capital and requires the usual precautions, expecially in small side-streets and the Puerta del Sol, a mecca for pickpockets. If you are robbed, go to the nearest police station to report the crime (*poner una denuncia*); the police are unlikely to find your belongings, but you will need to fill in a form for insurance purposes. It is always good to have a photocopy of your passport and extra passport-shots with you in case of problems.

After long years of easy-going controls, the law strictly forbade all drug-taking in public in 1992 and closed vari-

Newsstand at Cibeles fountain

ous bars and discotheques for this reason. Nevertheless, hashish (*chocolate/costo*) is sold blatantly on the street in certain areas (notably Plaza de Chueca and Plaza Dos de Mayo, especially at night). Cocaine is sold more discreetly.

There is a major heroin problem, which is the main cause of AIDS in Spain.

If you leave something of little value in a taxi, bus, museum or public place, it may be taken to the lost property office (Plaza de Legazpi 8, Tel: 5884346), but you need to leave a minimum of three days before you can find out whether it has been handed in.

For police emergencies, phone 091.

Left Luggage

Available at the **airport**, **Chamartín** train station, **Estación Sur** and **Plaza Colón** bus stations.

Toilets

Paying mobile loos are scattered around the city, but it is more usual to use those in a bar. You don't need to have a drink, but it is more polite to do so.

Post and Fax

Post offices (*correos*) are open Monday to Friday 9am–2pm and Saturday to 1pm. Alternatively – much quicker – buy stamps in an *estanco* (tobacconist) and use either a yellow postbox or red one (*express*). Telegrams are sent from post offices or by telephone (5222000). The ornate central **Palacio de Correos**, in

Calle Alcalá opposite Cibeles fountain (8.30am–10pm) is much faster than other post offices. Most hotels have a fax service; failing that, photocopy shops and stationers do, at a price.

Telephone

You can phone from a box (they have instructions in English, but are often out of order), from bars (more expensive, but more relaxed as you don't need the right coins), from hotels (up to four times the normal rate), or from public phone offices (**Palacio de Correos**; Gran Vía 30, Puerta de Recoletos 41), where you pay after the call and can use major credit cards. Ring 003 for Spanish directory enquiries, 9198 for European enquiries and 9191 for the rest of the world. To call other countries, first dial the international access code 07 followed by the relevant country code: United Kindom (44); Canada and the US (1); Australia (61); New Zealand (64); the Netherlands (31); Germany (49), then the area code without the initial 0, followed by the number.

If you are using a US credit phone card, dial the company's access number below, then 01, and then the country code. Sprint, Tel: 900 99 0013; AT&T, Tel: 900 99 0011; MCI, tel: 900 99 0014.

Media

The most important Madrid papers are: *El País*, serious information, pro-government, good foreign coverage; *ABC*, conservative and monarchical, good arts coverage; *El Mundo*, relatively sensationalist, a progressive political stance; *Diario 16*, also sensationalist, less critical of government and more progressive; *Ya*, Catholic, Madrid-based information. *Guía del Ocio* is a useful, if limited and staid, listings magazine.

Television

There are two state channels, TV1 (mass audience) and La 2 (documentaries, subtitled films, sport). Telemadrid, the local channel, has city news, football and films. Canal Plus shows new films and sports.

Casa de Campo amusements

Children

Madrid is very noisy at night, so make sure you have a quiet hotel room. The Spanish dote on children; they accompany adults to cafés, restaurants and fiestas, even very late at night, and are usually given a warm welcome. See also *Attractions*.

Disabled

Unfortunately, disabled people are not allowed on buses or the Metro. However, the city's five main museums all have disabled access.

Maps

El Aventurero, Calle Toledo 15–17, is an excellent map shop. The Michelin 444 covers a good area around Madrid; FALK plan is the best map of Madrid, if a little unwieldy.

Attractions

Descubre Madrid (Tel: 5882906), part of the Madrid tourist board, offers excellent specialist tours around the city, though these are mainly in Spanish. Madrid's main attraction, apart from its street-life, is its wealth of museums and galleries. Here it is possible to include only a small selection of these and other attractions not included in itineraries.

Campo del Moro (Puerta de la Virgen del Puerto; Metro Norte). Open daily 9.30am–sunset. Lovely gardens of the Royal Palace, also with the **carriages museum** (Monday to Friday 9.30am–5pm, Sunday and holidays 9am–2.15pm).

day 10am–3pm. Closed public holidays and August. Beautifully kept house of Valencian impressionist painter Sorolla, with his paintings, furnishings and garden.

Casa-Museo de Lope de Vega (Calle Cervantes 11, Tel: 4299216). Open Monday to Friday 9.30am–2.30pm, Saturday 10am–1.30pm. House of Spain's greatest dramatist, with its original 17th-century interior – still intact – including furniture and decor. A maximum of 10 people are allowed in at a time.

Centro Cultural de la Villa de Madrid (Plaza de Colón, Tel: 2756080; Metro Colón/Serrano). Art gallery, two auditoriums, and a café: there is always something going on.

Museo Lazaro Galdiano (Calle Serrano 122, Tel: 2616084; Metro Nuevos Ministerios). Open daily 10am–2pm. Exceptional private collection containing outstanding enamels, ivories, jewellery and Old Master paintings (Da Vinci, etc).

Museo Nacional de Ciencias Naturales (National Science Museum, Calle José Abascal 2, Tel: 2618600/4111328; Metro Nuevos Ministerios). Open Tuesday to Sunday 10am–6pm. Closed during August. Excellent exhibitions on the history and life of the planet earth; human evolution; minerals and man, plus temporary exhibitions.

Museo Romántico (Calle San Mateo 13, Tel: 4481045; Metro Alonso Martinez). Open Tuesday to Saturday 10am–3pm, Sunday 10am–2pm. Closed Monday, public holidays and during August. One of the most interesting small museums, in a 19th-century palace with fine furniture and paintings.

Museo Sorolla (Puerta General Martínez Campos 37, Tel: 4101584; Metro Ruben Darío or Iglesia). Open Tuesday to Sun-

Palacio El Pardo (Carretera de El Pardo *kilómetro* 8, Tel: 7360329). Buses (Alacuber) from Paseo Moret, corner with Princesa; every 20 minutes. Open Tuesday to Saturday 10am–1pm and 3.30–6pm, Sunday 10am–1pm. The 18th-century palace where Franco lived and King Juan Carlos was brought up, plus hunting park with wildlife.

Parque de Attracciónes (Casa de Campo, Tel: 4632900; Metro Batan). Highest rollercoaster in Europe, good ghost train, maxiscope screen, live concerts in summer. Global ticket includes two attractions. Open Saturday noon–10pm, Sunday and holidays noon–8pm.

Planetario (Pque Tierno Galván, Tel: 4673461; Metro Mendez Alvaro). The city's planetarium opens Tuesday to Sunday 11.30am, 12.45pm, 5.30pm, 6.45pm and 8pm (during winter Tuesday to Friday 5.30pm and 6.45pm only).

Real Academía de Bellas Artes de San Fernando (Calle Alcalá 13, Tel: 5221491; Metros Sol and Sevilla). Open Tuesday to Saturday 9am–7pm, Sunday 9am–2pm. Five centuries of Spanish painting, including works by El Greco, Goya, Alonso Cano, Zurbarán, plus print museum and temporary exhibitions.

Teleférico (Puerta de Pinto Rosales, Tel: 5417450; Metro Ventura Rodriguez). The popular cable car operates Monday to Friday 11am–2.30pm and 4.30pm–1am, Saturday and Sunday noon–2.30pm and 3.30–7.30pm. During October to March it operates Saturday and Sunday only.

Zoo (Casa de Campo; Metro Batán). Open daily, 10am–9pm (summer), 10.30am–7pm (October–April).

LANGUAGE

Castellano – what we generally call Spanish – is the official language, although four others (Gallego, Euskera, Catalan and Valencian) are used on an everyday basis elsewhere in the country. Most Spaniards have a smattering of English, but basic phrases are useful and the effort is appreciated.

SPORT

Most gyms require membership, so they are not really open to visitors. Jog in the parks (El Retiro, Parque del Oeste, Dehesa de la Villa), which are never crowded and significantly less full of fumes.

A swimming pool is a godsend in summer. **Canal Reina Isabel II** (summer only, Calle Sta Engracia 25, Tel: 4452000). The **Casa de Campo** (winter and summer, Tel: 4630050) has not only a pool, but also a tennis court that you can reserve. **Aqualung** (Puerta de la Ermita del Santo 40, Tel: 4634052) is a heated pool with waves. Open Tuesday to Saturday and holidays 10am–10pm.

Many *Madrileños* go skiing in the sierra when there is winter snow. The four main resorts (Navacerrada, Valcotos. Valdesqui and La Pinilla) are some 70km (43 miles) from the city and you can hire all equipment there. The best way to get there, to avoid traffic jams, is by train for Cercadilla or Cotos from Chamartín.

The main spectator sport is football, for which tickets are usually easily available on the day. Real Madrid's home is Estadio Santiago Bernabeu and Atlético de Madrid's is at Vicente Calderón, Puerta de Virgen del Puerto. There are also two excellent basket-ball teams worth catching: Real Madrid, who play at Puerta de la Castellana 259, and Estudiantes, at Palacio de Deportes de la Comunidad, Avenida de Felipe II 19.

USEFUL ADDRESSES

Customs: Calle Guzman el Bueno 137, Tel: 5543200
British Embassy: Calle Fernando el Santo 16, Tel: 3190200
French Embassy: Calle Salustiano Olozaga 9, Tel: 4355560
German Embassy: Calle Fortuny 8, Tel: 3199100
US Embassy: Calle Serrano 75, Tel: 276-3400
Tourist information offices: Torre de Madrid, Plaza de España, Tel: 5412325; at Chamartín railway station, Tel: 125-9976; at Barajas airport (international arrivals), Tel: 30588656
Barajas airport: Air ticket reservations, Tel: 5939966
RENFE **information and ticket sales**: Calle Alcalá 44, Tel: 3058544
Estación Sur de Autobuses: Calle Canarias 17, Tel: 4684200
Telétaxi: 4459008

FURTHER READING

The Adventures of Don Quixote, Miguel de Cervantes Saavedra, translated by J M Cohen, Penguin, London, 1950.
Madrid, Insight Guide, edited by Lucy Evans, APA, London, 1991.
Spain, Jan Morris, Penguin, London.
Ena: Spain's English Queen, Gerard Noel, Constable, London, 1989.
Fortunata and Jacinta, Benito Peréz Galdós, Penguin, London.
The Spanish Temper, V S Pritchett, The Hogarth Press, London, 1954.
Madrid, A Travellers' Companion, selected and introduced by Hugh Thomas, Constable, London, 1988.

Life on the tiles

Index

Photography **Bill Wassman** *and*
Page 79 **Wolfgang Fritz**
12, 15, 16 **José Martin**

Practical Information,
Toledo and Crafts itineraries **Juan Datri**
Editorial Assistant, additional research **Veronica Janssen**

*Thanks also to Maria José Lopez Palomo, Bruno Anguita (Patronato de Turismo de
Madrid), Blanca Fernandez (Descubre Madrid) and, among friends, especially Rocio Lopez,
the Pire Trives family, Anselmo Santos, Pilar Bittini, and Miguel Angel Arenas.*

Production Editor **Erich Meyer**
Handwriting **V.Barl**
Cover Design **Klaus Geisler**
Cartography **Berndtson & Berndtson**

INSIGHT *pocket* GUIDES

United States: Houghton Mifflin Company, Boston MA 02108
Tel: (800) 2253362 Fax: (800) 4589501

Canada: Thomas Allen & Son, 390 Steelcase Road East
Markham, Ontario L3R 1G2
Tel: (416) 4759126 Fax: (416) 4756747

Great Britain: GeoCenter UK, Hampshire RG22 4BJ
Tel: (256) 817987 Fax: (256) 817988

Worldwide: Höfer Communications Singapore 2262
Tel: (65) 8612755 Fax: (65) 8616438

"I was first drawn to the Insight Guides by the excellent "Nepal" volume. I can think of no book which so effectively captures the essence of a country. Out of these pages leaped the Nepal I know – the captivating charm of a people and their culture. I've since discovered and enjoyed the entire Insight Guide Series. Each volume deals with a country or city in the same sensitive depth, which is nowhere more evident than in the superb photography."

Sir Edmund Hillary

INSIGHT GUIDES

COLORSET NUMBERS

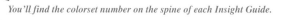

You'll find the colorset number on the spine of each Insight Guide.